Odes to Joy

Odes to Joy
and the Perils of a Single Society

Alastair Hannay

Published by
humming earth
an imprint of
Zeticula Ltd
Unit 13
196 Rose Street
Edinburgh
EH2 4AT
Scotland

http://www.hummingearth.com
admin@hummingearth.com

ISBN 978-1-84622-078-4

Acknowledgements

I owe thanks to a musical and ethnically erudite Brit Berggreen here in Norway and to my literary and poetic cousin Rowena Hill in Venezuela for help and support in the preparation of this book. My musical father must also be mentioned. One Sunday shortly after the end of World War II in Europe he took out his miniature score of Beethoven's Ninth and we both followed it while listening to the 1935 Felix Weingartner recording with the Vienna Philharmonic. Its cosmic proportions have supplied a frame for many musical adventures and its unforgettable finale provides a leitmotif for the severally related topics that crop up in the following pages.

Borre, January 2021

Contents

Prologue

'Everyone likes a singsong!'

Not everyone surely...

'Why would anyone *dislike* a singsong? It's a chance for merry-making and putting your troubles in that old kit bag. And it raises spirits, probably good for the soul too.'

Well, there are reasons: the deaf, for instance, or tone deaf, the disenfranchised, they can feel left out.

'No need to be able to sing to enjoy a good shanty.'

All right, but among landlubbers there are musical snobs who don't care for songs that enough people have to know to sing them together.

'Why care about them?'

There are others. Think of immigrants.

'Given the chance they'd join in.'

All right, but carousing with raucous revellers isn't everybody's cup of tea and the musical snob isn't the only dissenter. There's the dissident or provocateur. They can find something fishy in its harmlessness, the way people jump out of their everyday skins into a gung-ho nostalgic trance that leaves bystanders or bartenders gaping or cleaning glasses until it stops. Conversing drinkers can just look into their mugs.

'It isn't just pubs. It can be a busload of football supporters or the Last Night of the Proms. What's wrong with those?'

It's not just the noise factor or being unable to join in. You may have a singsong and even help with the piano but still feel uneasy: it doesn't just *sound* like escapism, it looks like it too. Join a choir instead of a discussion group and you are looking back instead of forward. Someone I know had qualms enough to write of an 'intense aversion to sing-along'.[1]

'All right, some wipe-the-smile-off-your-face philosopher.'

Well no, he wrote humorously and made it into a show, he even danced in it. Don't be too quick to assume. Just wait ...

'I'm all ears.'

With what it takes in between, assumedly!

---

1   Arne Berggren, *En intens motvilje mot allsang: Om kreative demoner og fordømt kreativitet* [An Intense Aversion to Sing-Along: On Creative Demons and Infernal Creativity], Oslo: Gyldendal, 2005.

1. Askancing Sing-Along

The contexts where people sing together are countless, some with good connotations, others bad. In mitigation of their misery convicts in chain gangs produced their own songs, while 'waulking' songs sung in Gaelic by Scottish women conditioning tweed and certain sea shanties were reminders of how to do things but also made doing them more enjoyable. Some singing together asks for an audience and its applause. There may be more joy at concerts in listening than having to follow the conductor and keeping the high notes. But these choruses, whether it's singing busloads of supporters or trained choirs, usually connect with better times, times gone or to come. Beethoven's rendering of Schiller's Ode to Joy, for instance, or those war-weary soldiers who came out of the trenches from both sides in World War I to sing Christmas carols before going back to kill each other. 'Three Cheers for the Red, White and Blue' had been spreading war fever in post-Victorian music halls not long before. Variety shows were said to be more effective recruitment boosters than the official exhortations by politicians with Etonian accents. Soon they would be marking the horror and the halls would be ringing to 'When the Boys Come Marching Home'.

The exultation projected in singing or felt by singers acquires a comfortingly ritual mode. It offers reassurances about a community spirit not always evident in the everyday. The images can be exaggerated. We sing the 'rocket's red glare', 'form your battalions' and 'rule Britannia' with a sneaking but carefully down-played jingoism. Small flags may wave but only momentarily in minds only dimly harking to what they have imbibed in school.

Such rituals can be little or much. Take holding hands while singing 'Auld Lang Syne' to remember the old while ringing in the new. Carols celebrating the Christ child can be squeaked out briefly at the door by small urchins for the sake of a coin, but in the Venezuelan and Andean La Paradura del Niño they are sung with texts following the played-out narrative which may be adapted to the celebratory occasion. Ourselves silent, we follow set-piece singsongs on television while a televised audience joins in with texts shown on *their* screen. Religious, heathen or just 'good old numbers', they offer a comforting cantabile in a staccato world.

But wait. What if sing-alongs became part of everyday, a fashion or habit, even a way of life, a requirement perhaps, like anthems and hymns before classes, daily exposure to equivalents of the Red Army Choir? Might not this unison focus on a glorified future or rose-tinted past raise just an eyebrow or two? Try this:

Already before the match began the difference between the two nations was evident. The loudspeakers bellowed out short excerpts of pop music, as in American sports arrangements. The South Koreans sang along. But the North Koreans, what did they do? They danced and joined in sing-along. Clapped and waved. Charming, yes, but perfectly coordinated in typical dictator-style, obviously choreographed. Even conducted. Crowned with the typically hugely overdone prearranged clapping and cheering.[2]

Although both were well organized, the South held to a tradition of listener-appreciation with roots in entertainment all the way to karaoke. The well-drilled celebration delivered by the North was pure advertisement. It gave an illusion of a nation on a fast track to social harmony. More to the point, where the Southern mix could give the impression of being aimed at individual viewers or members of a public, the Northern display was one of total immersion in collective and imitative action.

It is useful to reflect that forgetting selves was once thought to be the pathway to harmony in these our terrestrial lives: too much consciousness of self gets in the way. Removing this obstacle to universal concord was the aim of arrangements historically linked with those 2018 Winter Olympics to which that quotation belongs. Visions of wholeness could be enacted in which initiates subjected themselves to vicarious immersion in a cosmos to come or else in one lost and briefly to be recovered in participatory celebration. Consistently with the ideal of wholeness, these cults would be open to all, women and men, slaves and freemen, the old and young alike. Being cross-border arrangements, there were also guarantees of safe conduct to warring states for the duration, a small step for them but, in the light of the future, a big one for humankind.

In fact, however, their situation hardly differed from our own: few were in a position to attend

2   From the PyeongChang 1918 Winter Olympics,
      Aftenposten, Oslo, 17 February, 2018, my translation.

and the protection outside was sorely needed. It is unsurprising that, as well as being welcome, these spasms of joyful amnesia were institutional. Although our own extemporary get-togethers are but pale imitations of the dithyrambic abandon of Dionysian festivals honouring Homer's god of wine-preparation, at least as legend presents them, our extemporary choral get-togethers can provide some tepid trace of that elation.

Not more? Surely, wine can helpfully unfreeze the brain's deep-frozen and doubtlessly advantageous habits. Maybe too much 'self' means inhibition. Wine and song can still be a stimulant for fresh ideas for everyone, for women and men, rich and poor alike.

Quite so, but then is it not equally likely, or more, that a brain operating on its own and prompted by a less orchestrated environment will do better? Innovation and regimentation mix badly. New ideas are more likely to arise by leaving things to chance. Ask Woody Allen.[3]

This is just what that intense aversion to singing along is about. One thing is that togetherness, drilled or extemporary and however diverting, offers a misleading parody of real social harmony; another, and more vitally, is that sing-along not only stifles whatever creativity produced the songs but turns its back on the solitude it depends upon, these two, subjectivity and solitude being two sides of the same thing. That at least is the message my anti-sing-along writer left me with and whose substance I intend to investigate.

---

3   See Bradley Doucet, 'Point, Set & Match, Woody Allen's Ode to Chance', http://quebecoislibre.org.

2. 'In My Solitude'

What same thing, and how so? Well, note first that solitude is not, without further ado, loneliness. Being lonely is to feel lack of company, as when forced into lockdown in a pandemic. It is a felt deficit. Solitude is something we may seek, or else and paradoxically it is a kind of beginning we arrive at first by pushing things aside including flock-friendly habits like talking as if solitariness and loneliness are the same. Solitude isn't a matter of being left out, losing one's life-partner or friends. It is being oneself by oneself, and living in and from this oddly indefinable but sensibly mobile location we may all sometimes experience ourselves as no more than being. It is also what we mainly do our best trying not to be. If loneliness implies that company is to be preferred, solitude can be more than just retiring to the kitchen while the party goes on: it can be a ground zero where, like the clothing with which we cover our nakedness (also one meaning of 'habit'), what we share with others loosens its comfortable and comforting embrace.

Confronting 'us' at first as a deep well from which nothing can be drawn, that un-ground may turn out to be the well-spring of your life, the pool from which true selfhood flows, that is to say a selfhood that does not depend on how others see you.

Then again, though not unconnectedly, how natural it is to refer to 'we' when defending 'I'! Naturally enough, since enlistment in a social genus comes with birth. We bear our generic descriptions from the start, either consciously or as a matter of course too obvious to bring to mind. As we grow into our societies, we become some*one* by becoming some*thing*. Putting on a hat, any hat, a uniform cap, a helmet, wearing green and carrying a shotgun, all this pulls you into an ethnic or socially-defined genus, traditionally one that is comfortingly male if that is your native gender department. Even when rebellious, one still likes to be modishly so.

Since ever-widening generalities describe *what* we are, we might assume that the narrower the circumference, the closer we come to *who* we are. A point may be reached where all that is missing is an address or location of sorts. 'Itinerant' may do, '*x*' marking some spot in time and space momentarily inhabited by the happy or unhappy wanderer. After all, what else is there to be said?

Followers of the philosophical lore, especially the prestigious but no less precious canon of analytical philosophy, will be reminded of Bertrand Russell's path-breaking 'Theory of General Descriptions'. It allows us to talk of non-existent figures like the present King of France or fictional protagonists like Sherlock Holmes without committing ourselves to a belief in their actual existence. We do after all talk about the detective as if he did while knowing quite well that he didn't. By letting the description hang in the air we can pretend that, or just talk as if, there is or was a Sherlock Holmes. Likewise in the case of those famous but at times ambiguous figures we read about in history and myth. We talk of them with this matter of their existence on hold until – and it may never happen – told on authority that someone actually did or does or didn't or doesn't answer to their description. We wait, as it is said, for the 'existential quantifier' to inform us that 'there is an x such that s/he is, etc…'.

As for real existence, this itself is of course quite unreal. Popping the existential question doesn't even begin homing in on an existing someone. You might be led to suppose from the above that locating the 'I' of the 'x' is like penetrating to the core of a tropical cyclone where whirling masses of air at the perimeter revolve around a point-zero of utter calm. The 'I' is the eye of the storm and just as a geometrical point symbolized by a dot has neither width, length or depth, so here the self is drawn ever more narrowly to an axis to be identified only by what it is not.

The true existential situation suggests the opposite. The whirling masses emanate outwards from a centre involved in the expansion. What we are and what we may become are matters of where we begin and of how far we extend in the direction of the perimeter. As the energy or 'velocity' in a physical vortex decreases with distance from the centre, so too with the wider generic description: the less it says about who I am and what I am up to. Supplying the existential quantifier in real life is getting to grips with an actual walking, talking, hoping, enjoying, suffering individual at work with the prevailing winds and life's potential storms. Yes, there are descriptions that we consciously bear and we live within them, but *what* we are can never be exhausted by any list of these. There are of course some descriptions still to be fathomed or pointed out, and there are others for which we lack and may never have adequate labels. In these we remain immersed. But as far as we know *what* we are, we can never truthfully say 'this is *all* I am'.

A thinker from the nineteenth-century with some grasp of these things wrote of 'choosing oneself'. For him, the self to be chosen was the generic one we find ourselves being when we wake up to what we are. Birth deals us a hand of cards and while to our dying day the face values of some remain the same, others take time to show what they have to offer. There are leanings, temperament, abilities, gender and sexuality, and on top of that or underneath, a variably rigid or malleable social role.

So, while some plain ethnic properties recorded in our birth certificates and identity cards stay the same, others have their destiny in the future. How it turns out can be our own doing, less or more. Our nineteenth-century thinker insisted on the latter, and that is saying quite a lot: the 'self-aware' individual is not just conscious of being 'this definite individual' equipped with 'these aptitudes, these tendencies, these instincts, these passions, influenced by these definite surroundings, as this definite product of a definite outside world', no this individual 'assumes responsibility for it all'.[4]

We are all born in some section of a society with its own ways, whether traditional or radicalizing or both, and within the scope allowed by our given orbit we develop a history of sorts, a career perhaps, a skill as artisan or entertainer, as law enforcer or provocateur, scientist or inventor, road-builder or transport driver,

---

4   Søren Kierkegaard, *Either/Or: A Fragment of Life*, abridged and trans. Alastair Hannay, London: Penguin Books, 1992, p. 542.

midwife or funeral director, chemist or nurse, business executive or salesman. Everyone is, to some extent, a customer or client, and in societies that allow enough privacy to allow a space to be called 'public' that they all share, there is membership of that too. Looking at the cards, we can see what matters and what changes can be made in the dealt hand.

Not to do so is to look away. In his perhaps most famous book the same nineteenth-century thinker described two ways of looking at that hand. One is an opportunistic selecting that looks for a quick fix pay-off in pleasure, or in the 'Diary of a Seducer' a more general strategy for perpetuating the possibilities of self-satisfaction. The other way is an all-in approach that 'sees possibilities everywhere'. Not at all a matter of staking everything on winning the jackpot, it is to place your personal capital at the disposal of a universal ideal.[5]

Whether that ideal has any objective backing or any kind of authorization is, as far as you or anyone here on earth knows, up to the gods and therefore a matter for you yourself. It is up to you and you alone to go along with it, if it is what you want to believe and dedicate yourself to believing. You may wish that

---

5   *Either/Or*, pp. 542-543, where it is also said that seeing oneself as a 'product' of the surroundings etc. and choosing oneself as such a product is also in a way to produce oneself. As a product, however, this isolated 'I' is 'at that same instant 'in absolute continuity', that is to say with the world of which he or she is a product. In choosing one's self and taking on the civic life as the way to realize the ideal, the personal life of an isolated individual is 'manifested' in a 'higher form', higher than any who think of Robinson Crusoe as being isolation's true representative (p. 553).

in the world everything went together and that there was some pay-off for getting it to do so, and you may even feel strongly that it is right and 'written' to wish and work for it to be so. But your basis for that feeling is to be found only in whatever gives you a sense of its need, whether separation, loneliness or fear of losing the security of a home, or perhaps a general and generous sense that all of us should feel at home. To see it in that way is up to you.

According to that writer, if the self that is chosen in that second way has the ideal already implanted in it as something 'given' in the sense of being part of the property 'as is', then that self has not been chosen as it really is and therefore not been properly chosen. That is to say it has not been chosen in a sufficiently radical way. You have packed something you need into a self with that application already downloaded and choose without having the added risk of choosing that addition.

Interestingly in connection with our inquiry into solitude's role in creativity, our author has it that by 'withdraw[ing] from the surroundings' in a way sufficient to allow this choice, the individual's sense of itself at the moment of choice is one of the 'most complete isolation'.[6]

Whether or not this isolated and 'abstract' self that is able to choose itself in its 'concretion' actually does so, its 'self-awareness' is there for the taking or refusing. Not only that, barring insanity, any escape from this 'I's transcendence, any attempt to bury oneself in the descriptions one exemplifies, is impossible. Budding actors may try their best but knowing that it is an act is part of their profession. Jean-Paul Sartre has an example of someone doing their best to do away

---

6   Ibid., p. 542.

with the thought that it is a put-on. Read how Sartre's waiter would see himself if aware of its impossibility:

What ... I attempt to realize, is a being-in-itself of the café waiter, as if it were not just I that give my duties and the rights of my position their value and urgency, as if it were not my free choice to get up each morning at five o'clock or to remain in bed, at the risk of being fired. As if from the very fact that I sustain this role in existence I didn't transcend it on every side, as if I did not constitute myself as one *beyond* my position. ...[7]

The approaching step 'a little too quick', the head bent 'a little too eagerly' forward, the expression and voice 'a little too solicitous', all of this we can recognize as an act. It belongs with a repertoire that includes the superior politeness a waiter can show when having to please boorish and ignorant customers. But what we are specially to note in this case is the 'quickness and pitiless rapidity of a thing'. In making himself into some*thing* this waiter is in the 'mode of *being what I am* not ...'. It is a kind of self-deception that cannot deceive that Sartre famously calls 'bad faith' (*La mauvaise foi*).

With 'waiter' and 'customer' at one end of the scale and perhaps 'believer' and 'atheist' (or now more topically, 'liberal' and 'socialist') at the other, along with endless possibilities in between, such general descriptions provide tailor-made or cut-and-dried categories all well suited to feeding an inclination to immersion in a group. In an age of 'identity politics' we face a rapid multiplication of such conscious divisions.

Today the fragmentation into inter-defining groups

---

7   *Being and Nothingness* [*L'Etre et Néant*], trans. Hazel Barnes New York: Philosophical Library, 1956 pp. 98-100.

representing ethnicity, class, demography, sexual orientation, social rank or political attitude is not only 'normal', it is also heralded as necessary if social engineers are to clear the way to a more fair and unified future. By being brought to our notice, imbalances and unwanted differences are there for those who see the way to replacing them with a frictionless equilibrium to manipulate. The more we let divisions or oppositions and much else at a narrower level generate clear descriptions under which we are divided, the better able we (or those engineers) are to bring well-directed criticism and social expertise to bear on an unstable and insufficiently human social order.

Logically, however, that is close to nonsensical: a self-sustaining network of competing first-person plural identities lacks any point from which a vision of universal unity can emerge. Like the Messiah, the engineers must come from elsewhere. That is perhaps the disturbing message of Christianity. We need something more than we are born with. Yet, inspiring though it may be, universal fellowship as traditionally proclaimed in churches and celebratory odes put to music are still either just nostalgia or vain and potentially hypocritical rituals ungeared to real life, capable only of giving a further lease of normalcy to the *status quo*.

Practically, and more to the point, it can be no more than what philosophers call a 'regulative idea' or 'principle', an impossible ideal but one capable of governing idealistic moves and strategies designed to encourage at least an approximation. It may be helped negatively by natural disasters and other dire events that bring people together. After a Florida shooting, the United States briefly becomes a 'large family'. In smaller nations the achievements of a sports hero are shared by compatriots and can, as one newspaper put it, 'move the boundary' for what a countryman can do while they were all asleep.[8] In one sense it is a platitude. The sportsman comes from that country and, yes, no one from that country has done it better (in this case down-hill skiing). But the hint is that the honour is shared with those with a similar passport even while they slept.[9]

Would recent non-ethnic immigrants be included there? One may wonder. Naturally enough, one of one's own finding a place on the podium matters to a small nation and failure can cause a nationwide groan. It is also no secret that internally fragmented and disunited nations have had their inner diversity protected over centuries by the threat of war. Well-advertised engagement abroad can be in the economic interests of the nation but, in addition, by keeping the flag flying it binds together a heterogeneous 'public'.

The reality is vividly illustrated in the fiction of George Orwell's *1984* with its narrative of a totalitarian state kept as one by fake televised reports of hostilities on all sides and with a controlled media-language adjusted accordingly. Just as school massacres and terrorist attacks unite a people in short-lived horror at what might happen next door, so too can dips and debits on the scale of national pride be cured by refocusing our identities away from those rapidly

---

8   'Mens du sov, flyttet Aksel Lund Svindal grensene for hva som er mulig for en nordmann [while you were sleeping, Aksel Lund Svindal moved the boundaries for what a Norwegian can do]'. *Aftenposten*, Oslo, 15 February, 2018.

9   The language is presciently called 'Newspeak'. The novel was published in 1949.

whirling winds close to the multifarious storm centres of individual identity and finding common cause nearer the periphery. Headed in its direction we can begin to feel a national itch and find ourselves fetching out the national colours.

We can always wave a flag, yes, but bearing a banner for *humanity* in the spirit of the above remark would have to be a response to some further danger. The real possibility of the end of the planet would do, an asteroid on course for Earth for example, or today and not implausibly the fear of Planet Earth no longer sustaining life.

That could of course take a nasty turn in the opposite direction and end with individuals fighting for what remains of diminishing resources. Here, as vividly presented in the *Hunger Games* film trilogy,[10] the operative motive is fear and a natural impulse to self-preservation that heralds distressingly dystopian scenarios.

---

10   In the first of four science-fiction films (2012-2015), children in a fictional projection of the USA are forced to appear in a live television show in which the only rule is: Kill or be killed.

3. That Embraceable 'We'

It isn't hard to conjure some unsavoury associations of an associative 'we'. Strutting military parades on national days, flawless robot-like gymnastics at the Olympic so-called Games, incarceration for not singing the Chinese national anthem as prescribed, compulsory standing applause on the general secretary of the Communist Party's arrival, that mutual hand-clapping as a head of state, whether president or general secretary, enters an auditorium filled with regimented hand-clapping party members and ingratiating underlings, or just party members, as all of them are.

Even on occasions designed only for the faithful, in a televisual world such fly-on-the-wall spying has become normal. It gratifies supporters even if it nauseates opponents, while the indifferent may find it merely comical. Yet the publicity has its function. It lets others see it as part of the game. Shown a hall full of applauding constituents, you are given the impression that if the walls were transparent, still more applauding supporters would come into view and potentially without end.

The power of unanimity is enormous if rarely visible. We may not even feel it when ourselves agreed: there is a sense of being steered in the right direction, of having escaped the anxiety of doubt, or of being led astray by the dangerous ideas of some renegade. Back on course with the many, we can relax as part of a normal momentum. That time-honoured slogan, 'safety in numbers', suggests that, being one of them, you yourself need have no thought of the power of unanimity. This can be its secret but also its danger. Being 'of one mind' is seldom if ever a good thing. It can easily imply that of two minds each is putting the onus of authority on the other. Or perhaps it is a matter of authority seen simply in there being two 'about' the same, when two separate minds arriving at the same conclusion would be more convincing. The difference is one that may be hard to detect. 'The nation agrees that war is a bad thing' can cause all heads to nod, but war being in our day something 'we' all (at least officially) want to avoid, the airing of such platitudes is close to uttering a tautology. Less a conclusion of a discussion on a matter of importance, this 'agreement' expresses a widely shared but unreflective sentiment. A politician might use the sentence in making a case for appeasement, but equally to excuse an expedient exception 'in these abnormal times'.

Another political 'we' makes more blatant use of image management. In a democratic society, and particularly in a large nation, candidates for the top job are more likely to win if they present an appropriately authoritative persona but also show themselves, when it counts, to be just as unholier-than-thou as other members of the constituency that their selection and election depend upon. Professionals call it 'creating a brand'. Even if sections of the media with an investment in the outcome are always on hand to help, some candidates have the talent or training to create their own brand. A candidate who is too obviously representative of a less than holy constituency may have the opposite task of convincing the voting public that she or he is up to the job. Whether Ronald Reagan or Barak Obama, Adolf Hitler or Donald Trump, the impression of oneness with the voting public, however achieved, is a potent political force with results foreseeable by those not taken in and, dangerously, left out. Political propaganda is a 'we' factory that creates its own empire and by monopolizing the channels of information it spreads its own lethal form of unanimity.

The 'we' embrace is also marketed for its practical advantages and even cites necessity. The economics of temporality tell us to 'move on'. In our complex modern societies saving time is close to being a universal principle. Decision by majority helps by providing steps in a ratchet-like progression: 'Now we can get on to the next question.' Note that this 'we' is not that of unanimity: points made by dissenters disappear in the shelves where protocols are stored and 'agreement' here is already secured as a procedural rule prior to actual discussion. In whatever way the rule was agreed upon, whether by listening to an oracle or through yet another majority decision, all are agreed that whatever scruples get a hearing, a majority decision will be accepted by everyone and the scruples duly shelved until political circumstances allow them to be brought to the table again later.

It would be hard to exaggerate the status of majority decision in democratic societies. Its roots are deep enough to give it a kind of sanctity. Beneath the mystique, however, is the simpler fact that democratic procedures are both time-consuming and engage a large number of people whose own time could otherwise be used in sustaining their own or the land's economy. It is a price that *has* to be paid.

Beyond that, too, there seems to be a general belief that agreement is preferable to disagreement. Sharing it is not reserved for democrats, far from it: dictators are keenly aware of the danger of dissent. But there are many reasons one might give for its prevalence. Experience tells us that squabbling is not just unpleasant, it is often destructive and can 'turn ugly'. Most of us share with others a settled view of life that tells us that, when all is said and done, the harmony we have is something we must keep hold of and do our best to expand. That it should do so on its own may be doubtful, something that history, and not least recent history, tells us. But with a sense of that need tapping into an undercurrent of good will assisted by international agencies devoted to world harmony, we may nevertheless feel we are on the way.

This sense of being on the right path might be wishfully misinterpreted as an addendum to evolutionary theory when applied to the human species as so far evolved. The urge to congregate can look like an advantageous mutation that has outplayed discordant tendencies in the struggle for survival. With those disadvantageous discards now in the evolutionary bin, we may appear to be on the right road to harmony.

According to evolutionary theory the opposite should be happening as surely it is. Increasing differentiation is theoretically to be expected and is indeed the picture we have of humanity today, where the multiplying of species is 'botanized' in terms of proliferating 'we'-embracing groups. For reasons suggested, the differentiation doesn't reach far enough to dissolve grouping altogether, leaving only singled out individuals: it stops where individuals classify themselves under some group or several not necessarily concentric groups.

One basic group is traditionally the nation. It is where the individual is born naked both literally and culturally. Being (as is implicit in the word 'nation' itself) also the place of birth and thereby enculturation, it is a natural stopping point and one that in a world of many such groups has had a defensive and, where necessary, also offensive function in preserving conditions in which we 'become' ourselves. Becoming oneself here is a matter of acquiring an identity in terms of a native environment. The self that one becomes in that environment, seen simply as its product, is as yet unaware of itself as able in principle to take on responsibility for its own composition. But when so aware, that self may appreciate the advantages and even necessity of such an environment. It may suspect that it is essential to the growth of human harmony quite generally, beyond the one particular environment of which it is itself a product.

Equally, products of such an environment may respond to their own shortcomings as selves with an exaggerated attachment to the home culture. Threats to its integrity by invasion and the lasting effects of occupation, if only in memory, and likewise immigration, can have the same consolidating effect without these reactions seeming on the surface to possess any obviously underlying pathology. The history of 'Sinn Féin' (translated 'we ourselves') speaks to the former; once the political wing of the Irish Republican Army devoted to liberating Ireland from

British control, it is currently a cross-border party devoted to the re-unification of North and South. That outcome requires the defusing of what many see as unnecessarily divisive group and particularly religious identifications. In its culturally more complex way immigration too poses that problem, as witnessed by the proliferation of hard-edged, save-my-culture activists opposed in professedly Christian lands to 'Islamifying'.

Behind it all, we see the nation as a nest in which fledgling selves are (to stretch the metaphor) forever tied umbilically to their native context. Some may be too strongly tied for the chord to be cut or sufficiently weakened for them to be able or inclined to reflect on its functions. When the connection appears to be neglected, they may become bitter or defiant. But whether dropouts, activists or great artists, they may also be in a better position to see things as they are. Social deficits may be the cracks needed to let through the light that shows an over-protectiveness in these nests, a longing to linger in them, or it can be the light that releases an insight into or vision, realistic or fanciful, of what humanity in its greater maturity might be. It is in any case easy to underestimate the hold our natural homes have on us.

4. On The Fringe

Suppose we use sing-along as a metaphor for society in the sense of what we feel we have and do in common with a heritage still more or less at our fingertips. Some people are happily left out of their own society's sing-along. Not everyone is so dependent on filling the social slots they have been allotted. While some available niches are exclusive enough for those inhabiting them to be able to shrug off the identities that would otherwise cling to them, others due to some unusual trait, for instance a marked talent, have no need or less to bother about there being a place ready made for them: they acquire their own niche. Great artists are in this situation. To speak generically (as distinct from generally), they may be by birth or upbringing or both more socially naked than the everyday homemaker and breadwinner, and thus correspondingly exposed more than these to their own abstract selfhood. Lacking the temperament and doubtless in some cases the ability to conform, they face a void they alone can fill by exploiting their idiosyncrasy. If lucky, they may have a special talent to work both on and with.

Could this, then, be where the link can be found between those two sides of the alleged same thing that sing-along is said to erase, subjectivity and creativity?

On the surface that seems unlikely. Personal creativity if significant can lead to asocial if not antisocial behaviour, and if asocial then, most likely, to its own parallel countercultures, in other words, further group differentiation within a society. But we may also wonder whether creativity is needed. Isn't innovation enough, fixing things as we go along, or when it comes to making technological progress invention, new *ways* of doing things rather than new things to do? Surely what counts most is making the best of our abilities for our own good and that of others. The world, our world, has to be kept going , 'sustained' as we now say when consumption is outpacing production and nature ravaged in the attempt to keep up the supply of 'raw' materials. How in any case can solitude or isolation help in bringing harmony to a world where discord appears to be endemic? After all, we are social animals, are we not? There can be no future in going it alone.

Creativity may strike us, first of all, as a feature of individuality to be found among outsiders, people cultivating lives of their own, making their own niches with but a tenuous regard for the commonweal. Artists are creative in their own sphere, but their inspiration has on the surface little actual or intended social impact. Yes, Goya has his 'Disasters of War' and Picasso his 'Guernica', but even if these paintings bring home the horror expressed in their frames, they offer no help in eliminating its sources outside those frames. The works fascinate rather than inspire an electorate in any way that would lead to effective political measures. The only artists that directly affect our daily lives are architects whose grandiose creations celebrate wealth or victory, or in the case of a Le Corbusier, a Frank Lloyd Wright or a Mies van der Rohe monuments to their own skills often in the shape of impressive skyscrapers, skills that when it comes to drawing up habitable homes for the poor only get in the way.

Of writers, Orwell is already mentioned. The novel as a genre itself began as political and social comment. Think of those pioneer novelists: Swift, Defoe, Sterne, Fielding and Richardson. Their personal creativity could engage and stimulate a social conscience in those literate and to some extent therefore still politically influential sections of their societies. Nowadays, with approaching universal literacy, the genre has largely depoliticized itself and succumbed to the profitmaking dynamics of a society in the grip of market laws and an understandably time-out thirst for recreation among the readership. The market itself obeys principles closer to crowd psychology than decision theory and much current literature is designed to take our minds off actual danger and disaster or else to caricature or glorify these in safely historical drama.

What claim, then, can writers, or artists in general, have to provide or contribute to what one artist has called 'the creative spirit of a society'?

The words are those of the Australian singer, composer and author Nick Cave.[11] They suggest we should ask about music too. Here, the spectrum is enormous, encompassing topical ballads, protest songs as well as the perennial Hallelujah Chorus, both satanic Black Metal and Bach Cantatas, jazz in all its forms and folk music in its world-wide diversity. Music can also be a background that we hear without listening, when imposed sometimes so much so as to make us crave the silences it seems designed to fill. And then there is the variably memorable and multi-genre

---

11   See note 14. He also uses the expression 'creative soul of society', aptly in view of remarks on p. 76 below.

world of popular music with its never-ending series of currently celebrated pop stars. Some are genuinely artistic geniuses, but as part of the participatory syntax of their performances the rapture they receive tends to be indiscriminate. The same goes for the response to so-called serious or 'classical' music, though in the more controlled environment of a social occasion reserved as it is for a niche of aficionados, the rapture tends to the decorous apart from the now less frequent intrusively egocentric 'bravo'. Although much if not most classical music has been written with a decorously or enthusiastically listening audience in mind, to those for whom the social occasion means less, the music itself may mean more if listened to alone at home.

5. Self-Sealing Society

The target of Cave's remarks is the so-called Cancel Culture (or 'Call-out Culture') that ostracizes figures who express opinions counter to a prevailing code of correctness. It is a culture that to good effect emphasizes the equal rights to recognition of neglected enclaves in society, but blasts those (especially those with a voice to be heard) who dare say anything that dents the new facade of acceptance.

Society has several ways of reacting to criticism, whether it is seen as constructive or destructive. As noted, one of these is to listen to the criticism but as time goes by to assimilate its own more palatable version within the current social ethos. It allows the society to assume that it has learnt the lesson and is now in a position better than that of those contemporaries to grasp the point of it. Quite possibly, the real point of the criticism has been conveniently lost.

Another response is to avoid the issue altogether by providing a place in history or a public stage that presents the critics as respected figures to look back on with pride. Martin Luther King has his statue and place in US history but discrimination against Afro-Americans goes on. And although it was to lasting effect that the more truly historical Martin Luther pinned his message to a church door, other than in clothes, words and stylized ritual there is less difference now between Protestant and Catholic than was printed on that message, and much less than represented in the deadly symbols these have become in the cause of 'restoring' to a homeland a largely imagined original integrity.

Political correctness operates like a puncture repair kit. The needle prick of insight into what has been left out is covered over with a new patch of 'we'-ness: the 'we' of egality. It is a form of equality that looks away from difference to focus on what conditions members of a population must satisfy in social and political respects if they are to be included in the social mix. The concerned embracers themselves feel the better for their moral maturity when compared with those historical heroes commemorated by statues, and whose success was fuelled by slave labour or by other dehumanizing forms of exploitation that also dehumanized the dehumanizers. In toppling the statues, they may be proud of their membership of an enlightened society but while toppling a statue too quick to assume that at the time they would have been any better.

More to the point, that nineteenth-century thinker referred to earlier once wrote that this egalitarianism was 'the lowest kind of levelling, since 'levelling always corresponds to the denominator in terms of which all are made equal', and it is not this that makes an 'essential human being'.[12] It is a quick-fix remedy in which a morally embarrassing pinpoint is stopped and the smooth surface saved or recovered, the social

12   Søren Kierkegaard, *A Literary Review* (Two Ages,
      Reviewed by S. Kierkegaard) , trans. Alastair Hannay,
      London: Penguin Books, 2001, p. 86.

media playing their inquisitorial part in preserving the egalitarian facade. Anyone, any celebrity in particular, expressing the slightest doubt about the correctness of a latest addition to the identity collection is pilloried or 'called out'.

This self-sealing function makes it look as though society were enjoying a beneficial evolutionary mutation. We are told that, since we are social animals, a social life is for us 'natural', we need each other. That can seem too obvious to need saying. When a general lockdown is enforced to cope with a pandemic, our dependence on company becomes glaring. Any social amusement like a sing-along in such a case is a felt want. In this social limbo, the kindly thought of all those similarly affected might even generate the inspiring prospect of everyone holding hands to sing an Esperanto equivalent of 'Auld Lang Syne'.

When social isolation occurs in more normal circumstances we tend to think of it in terms of pathology. It can take many forms, but typical of modern society is the sense of having nothing to offer. To a sense of being superfluous in this way despair is one response. But it is one with no aim in sight and for which a society provides its own 'homecoming' in the form of counselling, hospitals and graveyards. Another is defiance, and there is always a group here, however peripheral or engaged, from religious sects to terrorist organizations or a combination of both, that is ready to receive new acolytes.

Lying in wait for a wider population of those sensitive to their social invisibility are the social media. Here, anyone feeling the world is paying them too little attention can become however anonymously the virtual centre of a cyber-space browsing public. The anonymity even frees them from the usual inhibitions of interpersonal communication, such as politeness and a willingness to hear others' points of view.

And yet the alacrity with which we reach for our mobile phones when confined with others in public spaces can make us wonder whether, as with the tornado, the picture here too should be reversed. The need that so many have to escape acknowledgment of the near presence of fellow travellers may indicate to the psychological observer how near we are to that inescapable solitude of the true human beginning. Looking as so many now do, as though they were mini-Atlases, into the echo chamber of their hand-held world-bubbles, whether they realize it or not, they can be thought of as hovering on that threshold with their backs still turned to that empty space.

Although the strategies of the misfit acquire a pathological look when seen as responses to a sane society which through no fault of its own may not have parts to offer everyone, these moves are easily interpreted as the more visible signs of a prophylactic function played by society itself: a way of protecting individuals from themselves. If that is so, then we are all engaged in humanity's desperate attempt to provide for itself a functional home.

It seems clear then that 'social animal' can be given a pathological as well as a natural reading. Although it is in human nature to seek company, human nature is not enough: it leaves us without a natural home or habitat. That, too, is natural enough, it is the way evolution has taken its randomly guided path. It has driven us out of nature, at least to the extent of being able and forced to evaluate our own position concerning how we find ourselves placed. It is not enough to say that tool-making and shelter-building and providing food are the 'natural' consequence. These occupations conveniently sublimate a sobering thought expressed by one exceptionally well placed to have it. Like us, but for the Son of Man more evidently so, there is no natural 'where' on which we can lay our heads.

It wasn't the forty days in the wilderness that deprived this expert of a dwelling but, as he said afterwards when resisting the devil's suggestion that he should have turned the stones into food, the fact that one 'cannot live from bread alone'.[13] It suggests not that we need cakes as well but that our 'abstract' selves should accept in the cards placed in their hands a chance to contribute in our own persons to the world's improvement. The assumption is that perfecting the state of humanity is 'on the cards' that have been dealt to us in life. The alternative is a nihilism giving us a free hand to make the best of it in whatever way *we* choose.

Yes, nihilism. That might be the feeling of being as nothing beneath the stars. Milan Kundera has written of the 'unbearable lightness of being' as a sense of hovering over a world free of commitments and responsibilities or gazing at its demands as at a shop window. Looking up at the starry heavens in awe, Immanuel Kant decided that the clue to its divinity was to be found in his pocket, or 'breast' as he himself put it, in the form of the Moral Law. A professedly godless Bertrand Russell, on the other hand, saw both the splendour and ourselves in the lesser light of inhabitants of a minute orb in a cosmic side alley. For Russell, though, there was something splendid and

13   *Matt* 4:1-11.

worth preserving in this little bazaar: its culture and the facts and promise of civilization – cosmic anomaly no doubt, but a jewel all the same and with a value all of its own.

Today negativists, nihilists, realists, the disenchanted, or whatever you call them, see it otherwise. Less a pearl in the oyster of space, our little globe is better seen as a heroic if cosmologically puny act of defiance. From the wheel to the cuckoo clock, from moon-landings to the home-based wonders of cyber-space, civilization and its history are mankind's fist thrust defiantly, and at times spitefully, at the vast nothing.

Is that perhaps the deeper subtext of those lofty spires that point towards heaven: not antennae aspiring to the eternal but rudely pointing the finger – in vain of course, for what realist would not die of shock if there came a response?

Staying inside our cultural cocoons is understandable. We do it in ways that seem progressive or reactionary. 'Black lives matter' aims at bringing a victimized group into line regarding treatment and (or in spite of) legal rights with a dominantly white population as the norm. Sexual harassment, gender revision, animal abuse, the exploitation of nature itself, and not least language management in the light of recovered history (how long will 'negro spirituals' be found in the song catalogues?), all of these 'disclosures' find their bandwagons with corresponding opportunities for censoriousness and allegations of 'inappropriate' behaviour.

Opponents, on the other hand, see it as introducing a veneer of sameness that pushes real cultural difference into the background. It talks of a multiculturalism while preaching conformity and threatens to deprive people of a heritage to which their images of selfhood are closely bound and from which they are dangerously separated. For some objectors it is not just a sense of belonging that political correctness undermines, it is the very ability to think afresh. Far from moral enlightenment, the new sense of propriety with its added messianic tones takes bourgeois complacency to a new (and low) level:

> Political correctness has grown to become the unhappiest religion in the world. ... Its once honourable attempt to reimagine our society in a more equitable way now embodies all the worst aspects that religion has to offer (and none of the beauty) – moral certainty and self-righteousness shorn even of the capacity for redemption.[14]

How, in the expression of the author of these words, can 'the creative spirit of a society' help to redeem us? From what and where do we find this spirit? And if we do find it, where does creativity's claimed link with subjectivity come in?

We still have a way to go, and as for that, what if anything have religion and redemption to do with it?

---

14   'Nick Cave, "cancel culture is bad religion run amuck,"' https://the guardian.com/music/2020//12/nick-cave-political correctness >

6. Tremors Below

The suggestion is that the sources of social renewal must be found among those whose creative imaginations have not been crushed by daily routine and the requirements of a viable economy and normal life. Whether we are thinking of Leonardo de Vinci or Woodstock, it is to a churning cauldron of new ideas, trends, styles and ways of life beneath the parroted rhetoric and cheap back-biting of politics we should look in our society for an injection of creativity. The metaphor of an underground experimental kitchen comes to mind. New recipes are tried out and the results of some exotic combinations find their way to menus tasty enough for people upstairs to improve their eating habits.

On the face of it that seems unlikely. Art can startle and by spiting current codes of decency its practitioners as well as their products may provoke disgust, at times deliberately. But the explosive potential is defused from the start. Art is there to be appraised on aesthetic grounds and any discomfort that is intended is cushioned by the very context of its presentation. Rather than causing rage, new and dangerous art is savoured for its impertinence and, yes, creativity. It may be true that the typical targets of satire are politicians, but along with caricature, and although the latter can cause serious social mayhem, in general it rarely jumps out of the circus ring of entertainment.

That may seem an underestimation of the influence of art on the world's future. The symbolism in Wagner's operas with their strong appeal to feeling had an influence not only on the focus and painting habits of impressionist and post-impressionist painters in France and elsewhere, which is a cul-de-sac as far as political influence goes; its abstract motifs also gave mythical depth to nationhood, something that in the case of Wagner's own nation has left its lasting imprint on our world. But it is harder to find positive political effects of artistic creativity. There are classic examples on offer. Like its original, John Gay's ballad based *The Beggar's Opera*, Brecht and Weil's *The Threepenny Opera* in the current context of socialism versus capitalism satirised politics and injustice.[15] The Nazi takeover followed only a few years later and although Germanic art (Berlin. München, Berne, Vienna) with injections from Russia has from the beginning of the twentieth century been astoundingly creative in its exploration of the aesthetics of colour and music, proliferation of images, the breaking of social taboos, and in its satirical recognition of their own nations' failures as well as humanity's, its contributions are framed in a socially inspiring but still politically hands-off atmosphere of wry honesty over the past, and with an inviting emptiness in the present, to be filled with uninhibited creativity in the world of art itself. There

---

15   The text of *Die Dreigroschenoper*, from 1928, was an adaptation of the original attributed also to Elisabeth Hauptmann, who was also the translator. The ballads were originally designed to be sung by the audience.

are no obvious implications for the future, unless it is a return to the old cry of anarchy.

There have been serious attempts to politicize art appreciation. John Berger, himself an artist, presented a television series 'Ways of Seeing' (1972) which with its Marxist flavouring of aesthetics encouraged audiences to see the political realities embedded in familiar artworks usually appreciated for their beauty and the painter's skills. Ernest Gombrich's *Art and Illusion* (1960) preceded him and before that André Malraux's *Les voix de silences* (1951). In Germany Theodor Adorno did the same for music on an even wider scale, also with a predominantly Marxist slant but shaded on either side by Hegel and Freud.

Yet these moves to bring a sense of participation to the art-viewer have little influence on the societies of which only a small and intellectual segment takes notice. When it does so, any usefully creative insight quickly evaporates in the hothouse of intra-mural debate.

Some more widely engaging topic is needed to bring about essential change, one closer to everyone's home, for instance as hinted earlier the fragility of the climate and a real risk of non-survival. There, however, it is not the responsible individual we would find motivated to emerge from the group to inspire political change. A primal urge to protect the family and at worst save one's own skin would make its bow.

So why not go to the artists themselves? With their ties of environmental self-identification sufficiently relaxed, artists are in a better position to sense what a society lacks and can give expression to it in their works. Such relaxation can of course have as many causes as faces, for instance psychic or environmental, upbringing, a difficult childhood, or prolonged illness that loosens the close ties that are the usual sources of generic identity. What saves them is the confirmation potential of an early spotted talent or not least a self-confidence that creative activity can itself do much to reinforce by intensifying one's self-image.

Strangely, or perhaps not, the loneliness that some 'deprived' artists have undergone has induced a solitude that in turn inspired a sympathy and solicitude for the human race, which then finds expression in their art. This, at any rate, has been said of that inventive expressionist, Vincent van Gogh.

Penniless and feeling his faith destroyed, van Gogh, at one time diagnosed as a manic depressive, sank into despair and was shunned by his companions and friends. 'They think I'm a madman', he told an acquaintance, 'because I wanted to be a true Christian. They turned me out like a dog, saying that I was causing a scandal'. It was then that van Gogh began to draw seriously, thereby discovering in 1880 his true vocation as an artist. He decided that his mission from then on would be to bring consolation to humanity through art. 'I want to give the wretched a brotherly message', he explained to his brother Theo. 'When I sign [my paintings] "Vincent",' it is as one of them.' This realization of his creative powers restored his self-confidence.[16]

---

16   www.britannica.com Vincent van Gogh, Biography, Art
      and Facts.

7. The Beethoven Case

Another 'van' comes to mind: Ludwig van Beethoven, whose entitlement to the prefix had as little to do with nobility but who, like Vincent van Gogh, lays claim to another and less institutional elevation. As already mentioned, he plays a large part in Milan Kundera's novels. There the focus is on the late Beethoven. As a commentator has it:

For Kundera it is clearly the late Beethoven that counts. [The] so-called middle period, where his most played works were composed, such as the third and fifth symphonies, the 'Pathetique' and 'Appassionata' piano sonatas, the fourth and fifth piano concertos and violin concerto, do not interest him – at least in the books. Kundera sees the late Beethoven as the great solitary bearing his fate, as Atlas bears the heavenly vault on his shoulders. Heavier it can hardly be.[17]

Heavy indeed. Weight as 'a metaphor for fate and responsibility', as a commentator notes, is a theme in Kundera's *The Unbearable Lightness of Being*. The lightness already referred to is that of someone 'confronted by so many options' that he 'throws import

17   Egil Baumann, 'Kunderas Beethoven',
        'Musikkmagasinet', *Klassekampen*, Oslo, 19 October,
        2020, p. 6. My translation.

to the wind'. Quoting a phrase that Beethoven uses as a musical motto in the final movement of his own last string quartet, *'Es muss sein!'* ('It has to be'), the novel's protagonist reads it as saying that the weight has been lifted from his shoulders.

You might ask how a heavenly-vault bearing Atlas analogue can be in one breath the late Beethoven and in the next an Atlas that has delivered all that is important to the winds. The phrase in the quartet answers another, asking *'Muss es sein?'* ('Must it be'?) With Atlas the model, you might expect the opposite response, that what has to be is a fate for which I now have taken all responsibility. So what was it that had to be and at the same time it being so might be such a relief? There are several possibilities. At this late time, Beethoven in failing health, *'Es muss sein!'* can be resignation to his impending death: yes, it must be, it is coming anyway. In the following spring it did.

Or was it 'Why worry any longer about bearing my own fate and it being the right thing to do?' The question would be adopting what the same commentator calls a 'hypothetical and critical stance', a 'philosophical' position asking subjects to 'name their world' and the way in which we can all learn to 'break through unreflective and ossified thinking'.[18] It sounds like the politically and culturally radical Beethoven. Could it be that, in this year before he died, the composer was putting his whole life and career in parentheses and reflecting on the outcome of a life dedicated, as Van Gogh's later, to bringing consolation to humanity

---

18   Randall Everett Allsup, 'Music Education as Liberatory Practice: Exploring the Ideas of Milan Kundera', *Philosophy of Music Education Review* 9, no. 2 (Spring 2001), p. 3.

through art? Is Beethoven saying 'Will it really get anyone anywhere? Has it even got me anywhere? Has it been worth it? 'Who knows, I must just let it be as it must.'

These weight-lifting stories are a trifle far-fetched, but they are also unnecessary and there are lighter versions of the motto's origin that can tell us more about Beethoven.

He had told his publisher of his difficulty in finding ideas for this final movement: 'I could not bring myself to compose the last movement ... and that is the reason why I have written the motto: *The decision taken with much difficulty – Must it be? – It must be, it must be!* –'. Exactly. He would not give up.

Only slightly less impromptu is the story that the motto came to him at a quartet party where one of the four parts was missing. Beethoven's rich host hadn't yet bought a ticket for the forthcoming premiere, and Beethoven jokingly but serious said the missing part wouldn't be supplied until he paid up for one. Also jokingly, the rich man asked, 'Must it be?', at which 'Beethoven laughed and dashed off a canon on "It must be! Out with your wallet!".'[19]

If true, that wouldn't be the first time a chance remark or idea took root to become a composition. Indeed, it seemed to be the rule. Nor would it surprise us more if as, according to another version, it was following an exchange with his 'abominable'[20] housekeeper that Beethoven solved the difficulty in question. The insistent '*Must* it be?' calls for something sharper much than an 'I guess so!' or 'Let's see!'. The appropriate

---

19   Jan Swafford, *Beethoven: Anguish and Triumph*,
      London: Faber & Faber, 2014, p. 918.
20   The epithet from Swafford, *Beethoven*, p. 991.

response is 'Of course, what did you expect?' The F-Major Quartet's final movement has been described as not just a 'fitting end to Beethoven's career' but as one of the finest examples of his humour in music'.[21] There is, or can be, an unmistakable lightness in *this* 'It must be!'. It refers to itself and is saying 'Here it is, there you see, I did it!'

This, we should know, is the same Beethoven who, thirteen years earlier after an associate – on completing with him the arrangement of a revision of the opera *Fidelio* – appended a note saying 'Finished, with the help of God', had scrawled in a large hand 'O Man [*Mensch*] help yourself'.[22] As usual, where Beethoven was concerned, it *had* to happen and he was the one to make it so.

It was all of twenty-four years earlier that a down-in-the-dumps Beethoven had written a testament, at Heiligenstadt outside Vienna in the form of a letter ostensibly to his brothers but never sent. In it he confessed to his on-coming deafness and spoke of going into seclusion to hide what in the public mind would be a serious set-back for an up-and-coming composer. He wrote of suicide.

That same suicidal year saw though not inconsistently a series of works that finally broke with the traditions of Mozart and Haydn within which he had begun developing his own style when first coming to Vienna. It included the 'Kreutzer' sonata for violin and piano and was followed by the 'heroic' period of the third and fifth symphonies to say nothing of the exuberant fourth. Beethoven had now become himself.

---

21   William Kinderman, *Beethoven*, 2nd ed., Oxford: Oxford University Press, 2009, p.366.

22   Swafford, *Beethoven*, p. 628.

But this period, which included the 'Pathétique' and 'Appassionata' sonatas, was still not the one with which Kundera associates the great solitary hero bearing the heavy burden of his fate.

What, then, was it that made the later period so different and the burden so much heavier? Or was it really lighter and even not unbearably so?

Irascible, outspoken, uncouth, ironic, humorous, a punster *in excelsis* and master of word association more generally, this was now also a composer and pianist who for nine years had been totally deaf. There was no world he had to listen to anymore with its stupidities. As for applause, he had probably received enough of that. Respect for his audiences was not a strong point in any case. This was a Beethoven left to his own devices and now that actual humans had no longer to be entertained, with them devoted to humanity.

Withdrawn but not out of circulation, Beethoven was still to be seen on Vienna's streets, gesticulating and shouting as he rehearsed his latest musical thoughts. The philosopher and musicologist Theodor Adorno thought the deafness was a blessing that Beethoven might even have wished upon himself, the reason being that the sound of music in public places disturbed the inner process.[23] It must also have helped his creativity by insulating him from the noise of current musical convention.

There are parallels in other composers and artists, Schumann, for example, with a violin concerto said to show signs of brain damage due to syphilis. Knowing

---

23   Theodor W. Adorno, *Beethoven. The Philosophy of Music*, trans. Edmund Jephcott, London: Polity Press, 1998, here Fragments and Texts', trans Rolf Tiedemann, p. 31.

that the artist Willem de Kooning in later years suffered from Alzheimer, in the radical change and apparent disintegration in his later works, the art critics saw degeneration. An alternative appraisal would ascribe it to renewal due to release from the bondage of convention. It allowed the works to become spiritually more transparent.

To his contemporaries Beethoven's later music was an enigma and embarrassment. Uncensored by a once watchful editorial ear, the composer's renowned urge for novelty was now producing works that sounded like undeveloped drafts or even sheer guesswork. An earlier enthusiast who had conducted the earlier works, Louis Spohr, found that even these could not be 'preserved from error by guidance of the ear'.[24] To Adorno the lack of such guidance was its great secret and the reason why 'the late works ... are undoubtedly the most substantial and serious to be found anywhere in music'. As a reader of Hegel, Adorno even found here a kind of dialectic in which artistic genius generates an inner critique of the composer's earlier 'classicist works and takes the music to a higher level':

Beethoven's development gave expression to [a] feeling of dissatisfaction with the drapery, with the claim of classical totality. Critique here means simply to obey in the work the ideal inherent in the problem posed by the work; it is an objective critique arising from the compulsion of the subject matter, not from subjective reflection.[25]

---

24   www.spohr-society.org.uk. Passages in the middle period works were also 'rhapsodies of madness'.

25   Adorno, *Beethoven*, p. 190. Richard Wagner had already declared that Beethoven's creativity and genius had their source in his deafness. He compared Beethoven with Homer's blind seer Tiresias, who saw into the future, just

As we would expect, there was a subjective side too. The novelty can well arise from a musical mind unconstrained by reminders of what had been appropriated from classical models, but the critique was also that of a musical craftsman who had accumulated vast tonal experience and understanding and was able now to relive and transfer a closely focused wealth of experience onto the pages of a musical score. These latest compositions from the last three years of Beethoven's life were so compactly expressive of bitterness and humour, and of life's sorrows and aspirations, as to confound his contemporaries except for a select few with their ears and inner beings similarly tuned.

Franz Schubert's last musical wish before dying at the age of thirty-one in November 1827, twenty months after Beethoven, was to hear the Op. 131 quartet. Later, on hearing the first movement of what Beethoven declared to be his best composition, Richard Wagner said it was 'the saddest thing ever said in notes'.[26]

Sadness? That sounds a bit shallow. 'Troubled, sometimes turbulent and contemplative' might be better. If we are to ask what has happened to the triumphant joy of the Ninth's finale only three years earlier, the answer can be that we have moved on from a musical representation of the end of human strife to an inner vision of actual suffering and aspiration.

What would Beethoven himself make now of the joyous din of that Ode that he had set to music? At that time too, as he was actually doing so, it was only

as the deaf can hear what others can't. Richard Wagner, *Beethoven* (1870), trans. Roger Allen, Woodbridge UK: Boydell & Brewer, 2014, p. 109.

26   Swafford, *Beethoven*, p. 906.

in his inner ear that he was heating it. But might not its presence now, even there, be a hindrance to concentration? However inspiring, the time for ecstatic anticipations of a world freed of strife was over. The same goes for the over-the-top ardour of those words proclaiming universal fellowship. A vision cast in music like that can last only for the joyous moment of communication.

It was a more (let us call it) existential vision that inspired these works. Instead of campaigning for the cause of humanity in terms of a freedom understood in political terms as a release from oppression and tyranny as in *Egmont* and *Fidelio*, Beethoven's works now give expression to a freedom harder to pin down because it applied to everyone and meant letting go of any equivalent of Vienna's supporting scaffolding of clericalism, partisanship and a settled social hierarchy. The later music, a product of solitude, is that of humanity itself as of now, in its usually well-shielded essence and possibly if not presumably as it is everywhere and, as far as we know, always will be. It 'speaks' *from* this isolation and *to* an ideal of autonomy which, as one commentator notes, is a 'prerequisite of moral action or creativity'.[27]

May those words perhaps shed more of the light we are looking for on how subjectivity and creativity are two sides of the same thing?

---

27   Kinderman, *Beethoven*, p. 8.

8. Ordinary Humans

Van Gogh's last-hope mission was to 'bring consolation to humanity through art'. When putting his name to his works, it would be as 'one of them'. Half a century earlier we have this other 'deprived' artist expressing solicitude for the ordinary human being, at least to those with, let us say, the souls as well as ears to hear it.

As noted, loneliness may bring with it a sense of being superfluous, of having nothing to offer one's fellows. Ludwig van Beethoven seems never to have felt this way. No need for him to jump on some contemporary bandwagon already in motion like today's Jehovah Witnesses or Jihad. Rather, the isolation ignited a desire to show the world and himself what talent can achieve.

His own world, however, was the problem-filled one in which an ambitious father had propelled the eldest surviving son into local fame in Bonn as a potential new Mozart. The idolized mother died when he was seventeen and when an alcoholised and penniless father's death left the son to support his family, the talented young man was twenty-two.

He remained loyal to his origins and in an inborn as much as moral sense responsible for their welfare throughout his life. In those last years of works composed in isolation, he tried to take care of a nephew whose attempted suicide not long before his own death was doubtless due in part to the uncle's shortcomings in the area of human contact. As custodian of his own talent, and with a continual need to finance it, Beethoven had little opportunity to develop ordinary life skills and relationships even if he had the native disposition to do so. It was said of him, in his later years, that '[e]ven among his oldest friends he had to be humoured like a wayward child'.[28] Commissions from aristocratic benefactors, for whose social status he had little respect, and the need to compose potboilers on the way to pay for his keep, this was all enough to keep his musical mind focused on visions of a better world.

Of his actual childhood it is also said that it was one in which he 'did not truly comprehend the independent existence of other people'. But then '[h]e never really did'.

He reached maturity knowing all about music, from writing notes to selling them, but otherwise he did not know how to live in this world. In the ideals he lived by in his solitude, instead of human beings there would be an exalted abstraction. Humanity.[29]

It is also recounted that those in his circle could discern the 'generous, warm, world-embracing heart that lay under so much rage, cynicism, paranoia, solipsism, and human incapacity'. Unwilling or unable to appreciate the sufferings of others and out

28   O. G. Sonneck (ed.). *Beethoven: Impressions by his Contemporaries*, New York: Dover Publications, 1967, pp. 113-114.
29   Swafford, *Beethoven*, p. 39.

of contact with the world, you would think that, as a social dunce, this most humanitarian as well as creative of artists must be among the least able to contribute creatively to society itself. Beethoven was nevertheless worldly enough to be conscious of his social naïvety and is recorded as admitting to his publisher that his 'character' did not 'allow [him] to be 'distrustful'. [30]

The honesty and simplicity inherent in that remark may hint at a conscious desire to compensate for a felt lack of social graces by extolling humanity at large, an ideal projection of what was lacking in his own reality.

But there can be more to it. Schubert admitted that he had been so impressed with Beethoven's earlier works as to ask 'Who can do anything after Beethoven?' Unlike Wagner, for whom that opening Adagio of the late quartet meant overwhelming sadness, Schubert's own music, like that of Brahms after him, but increasingly more so the works of composers, such as Tchaikovsky, readier to let their hearts bleed in the music, speaks more directly from its source. There it is the composer speaking, the chosen one for whom talent also means hardship, with the music written to develop the individually expressive power of music itself and motivated by inner necessity. As for Wagner, not one to let his heart bleed in public if at all, his talent was to project feeling in stylized pictorial forms that could bestow on Isolde's troubles a grandeur far beyond the orbit of any normally beating heart.

Music, as any artistic medium, whether sound, colour or shape, or any blend of these, is a lingua franca in which an artist's insight and intuition can be shared independently of the context and cause of its origin. Provided enculturation allows familiarity with the

---

30   Ibid., p. 667.

medium, any relevantly tuned heart can grasp it: its availability is in principle worldwide. Of Beethoven it can be said that the musical language of his late works reaches widely because it digs deeply enough into the recesses of the human soul to reach a point where social fixtures become variables. Even if for some it can take a lifetime to appreciate the musical idiom, while for others it is beyond all reach, the appeal to a universal humanity from a composer with a sense of conflicts to which others turn a blind eye comes close enough to representing humanity in its universally existential condition. This un-ordinary (a more fitting description perhaps than the boundary-breaking 'extraordinary' or too indeterminate 'unusual') human being would be able to reach the ordinary human better than most ordinary humans whatever their cultural and social contexts.

1801 saw the premiere of the only ballet for which Beethoven wrote music, *The Creatures of Prometheus*. The width of its appeal is indicated by the fact that it was performed in New York as early as 1808. It was in fact the first of Beethoven's concert works to be heard there. In letter to a friend at the time of composition, Beethoven reveals that due to his unwillingness to let people know that he was becoming deaf, he had already for two years been keeping himself out of circulation.[31] The music itself, worlds away from those quartets to come, sounds nevertheless very much as though Beethoven enjoyed it himself.

It also served a purpose. The myth of Prometheus, who stole fire from heaven to give life to his two clay figures, is presented as an allegory of the birth of normal human beings. They emerge as such after the

---

31   Kinderman, *Beethoven*, p. 69.

Muses have infused them with music and knowledge of tragedy, comedy singing and the pastoral dance, as it happens the only kind of dance shared by the Viennese élite and ordinary folk at the time. It also warns of the dangers of Bacchic or Dionysian frenzy. The ballet ends with a heroic dance introduced by Dionysus and played to music now more familiar in refashioned form in the finale of the *Eroica* symphony. A point is made by the fact that everyone, including Apollo, takes part in the dance but the dance itself is led by the human beings to whose creation they have all contributed.

This ballet with its contemporary political message conveyed in an allegory can well claim to be evidence of a society's creative spirit. But there is some ambiguity in that expression: a society's creative spirit might be its ability to renew itself at the level of its own present political identity. Thucydides could write of Athens as 'the school of Hellas'.[32] A modern society is too internally heterogeneous and atomized to be able to educate itself. Rather than a feature of the society as a whole, this example from early nineteenth-century Vienna is of creativity lurking somehow in its interior. Aimed less at realizing the values of the Enlightenment in the Austria of the time, let alone Europe, the ballet is more like acknowledgment or a reminder of something already afoot. True, there is an extra creativity in the way that allegory is put to use here, as it had been so many times earlier and elsewhere. Jonathan Swift's *Gulliver's Travels* and the Greek tragedians come to

---

32   Thucydides, *The History of the Peloponnesian War*,
      trans. with introduction, marginal analysis, notes,
      Benjamin Jowett and indices, Oxford. Clarendon Press.
      1881, II, 41.

mind, and not least Aristophanes. If the *Creatures* didn't go straight to the point as in a work by Berthold Brecht, it at least appealed to the political intelligence of a literate population by putting demands on its knowledge and decoding powers.

The situation can be compared with a ticker text scrolling rapidly below a sluggish script recording actual political change. A society's subcultures usually survive on their own terms and at variable speeds denoted by 'canons' and national heritage in slow gear with passing fads and a constant renewal as popular stars racing past below. Far from hastening political change or cracking the surface of habitual thought and practice, the most active subcultures serve not only as work places for genuine talent but as insulated sanctuaries for the ill-adapted or frustrated who are looking for a social niche. The songs of protesters and rebels speak to a particular time and place and the response is to be found in those immediately affected. For others, the protest songs of rebels like Bob Dylan to Bob Marley, as of so many before and after, serve as absorbing and enthusing safety valves that may mitigate or confine the danger of any open discontent. Eventually they become collector's items and help to preserve rather than dissolve a longer-standing *status quo*.

It seems that it is only when discontent arises in 'ordinary' humans' driven to protest in sufficient numbers in the streets that it can threaten a 'regime', unless, that is, some outside power has the influence to do so or a faction from within. It may even win the day when led by an artist or writer such as Václav Havel. But the ability of artistic activity itself to bring about social and political change is not at all obvious and there seems little historically to be said for it.

On the other hand, a society that loses all sources of new ideas, trends, styles and ways of life, or for totalitarian reasons puts a lockdown on those sources that exist, can well be said to have lost its soul. The absence of any felt need of an undercurrent of belief in a world unified in its multicultural diversity is hard to imagine, but if it became a fact, it would empty the word 'humanity' of meaning. The writer, James Baldwin, insistent in his time on describing himself as a Negro, said that, 'if you examine and face your life, you can discover the terms with which you are connected with other lives, and they can discover, too, the terms with which they are connected to other people'.[33] He also said that in the end neither 'soldiers', 'statesmen', 'priests' nor 'union leaders', but only the poets, meaning 'all artists', 'know the truth about us'. Baldwin saw the artist's struggle for integrity as 'a kind of metaphor for the struggle, which is universal and daily, of all human beings on the face of this globe to get to become human beings'.[34]

The messages of myths and ballets can be ambiguous and can be interpreted or misinterpreted in ways that are divisive. But so long as there are articulate champions of human unity in diversity and provided the channels of communication are kept open, so that politically dangerous distortions of truth are open to inspection, perhaps the Promethean experiment may succeed even in the hands of ordinary humans.

---

33   Fred L. Standley and Louis H. Pratt (eds.), *Conversations with James Baldwin*, Jackson, MS: University Press of Mississippi, p. 21.

34   https://www.brainpickings.org/2016//04/13/james-baldwin-the-artists-struggle-for-integrity/

9. 'You'll Never Walk Alone'

What if that ballet's message is taken seriously and we assume that leading the human dance is a matter for human being in its ordinariness? If the dance includes everyone, the question is not how ordinary humans are going to lead the dance but how they are going to stage it. That might be the unworldly question of how to achieve a world without human conflict. More realistically and humanly, it is the question of how to approach an ideal world in which there is no *in*human conflict.

Whatever social, cultural, multicultural, national or international harmony is achieved, strife in some forms will surely remain part of the social order. Conscious competitiveness, as against the blind results of random mutation in nature, seems endemic to human life and in context even advantageously. Sibling rivalry is a case in point and generalized in the mollified form of organized competition, which is for us an inheritance from the Greeks, it is part of an everyday world of coloured scarves and caps. In sports, competition brings a healthy sense of challenge or triumph to the competitors and spectators are provided with some heart-warming excitement, also a chance to give full throated voice, yes, shout and even scream.

But also sing. And what is it we hear? 'You'll never walk alone!' The tradition began with supporters of the Liverpool Football Club when the song of that title topped the charts in 1963, sung by a local artist Gerry Marsden with the *Pacemakers*. It tells us 'when you walk through a storm' to 'hold your head up high' and not be 'afraid of the dark'. It became popular with supporters around the world.

With its hint of holiness and what can sound like a prospect of divine redemption, the song has the gravity and pathos of a revivalist hymn. For many Liverpool supporters, singing together in a common cause would be enough. It would be a refreshing escape from a humdrum life. But a sense of supporter solidarity can quickly supervene, and when the supporters on the other side join in too, we are on the way to something greater, a sense of brotherhood not only among football supporters but in our minds, and by extension, with all humanity. We might then envisage 'You'll never walk alone' itself joining hands with *The Ode to Joy*, Beethoven's setting of Schiller's *An die Freude*.

The supporter song became the anthem for minders and patients in the COVID-19 pandemic. The choral finale of Beethoven's Ninth was the hymn that celebrated the fall of the Berlin Wall in 1989. There, in what can be seen either as spontaneous *joie de vivre* in response to a moment in history or else as a slick propaganda move, 'joy' was replaced by 'freedom'. The effect was to distract attention from the more topical joy of re-united families, and it was this that engaged actual German citizens and was symbolically acknowledged in the formation of the orchestra, with its musicians from East and West Germany and the four occupying powers.

Freedom was obviously also a part of it, but freedom is a slippery notion and it is one thing no longer to be under a stifling atmosphere of mutual suspicion and having to toe the party line, but another to have the fall of the Berlin Wall heralded as a victory for liberal democracy as such. Those who shout freedom in that tone of voice typically refrain from naming the challenges that have to be met to achieve its benefits for a shared society, and the personal responsibilities involved, something that many will feel is typical of the ethos of nations still in the grip of the myths of their origins.

This was far from the only occasion on which Beethoven's choral finale has served political ends. It had been performed in its original 'joy' version to glorify the supremacist 'we'-ship of Nazi fascism, but also to protest the murderous Pinochet regime in Chile. It was brought to the attention of the Japanese by German prisoners in World War I and recently the Ninth was performed there with a choir of ten thousand where there were enough 'in attendance' to fill a stadium. It was labelled the 'Symphony of the World'.

It is ironic that, before the wall fell, East Germany had also cultivated Beethoven as its musical patron. The revolutionary strain to be heard in the 'Eroica' and Fifth symphonies harmonized with a belief in the humanizing effect of art, something that in its turn chimed with the Democratic Republic's belief in culture's ability to inspire unity according to its model. However:

> [b]eyond the sphere of official rhetoric ... Beethoven's reception was far more conflicted. As the promised socialist utopia failed to materialize

and the chasm widened between the rhetoric of revolution propagated by the party and the realities of life in the socialist state, Beethoven was approached increasingly not as an iconic statesman but as a vehicle for exploring the problematic position of art and the artist in East German society.

A film produced in East Germany, Horst Seemann's 1976 *Tage aus einem Leben* [Days from a Life] puts a finer point on some of our earlier remarks:

[T]he opening scenes ... cut between a live performance of Beethoven's 'Battle Symphony' and a gory re-enactment of the Battle of Vittoria itself. Far from heralding the symphony as a revolutionary force ... this juxtaposition of concert hall and battlefield exposes the fallacy of the Beethoven myth. Graphic images of wounded and dying soldiers sit uncomfortably with f r a m e s of the concert audience, who clap delightedly in response to the music and eat chocolates as they listen. Art serves here not as a harbinger of political change but simply as a mode of entertainment.[35]

That East German artists saw Beethoven under another spotlight is testimony to the creative skills of propagandists, but it also attests to the difficulty if not impossibility of determining the intentions and achievements of an artist beyond those of developing a creative talent and some guesswork on our part as to what influence current events may be found in their products. Is it not possible, for example, to see Beethoven's setting of the 'Ode to Joy' in the narrower

---

35   Elaine Kelly, 'Beethoven and the Berlin Wall', oup.blog. com. See Elaine Kelly, *Composing the Canon in the German Democratic Republic: Narratives of Nineteenth-Century Music,* Oxford University Press, 2014.

light of his clearly stated dismay at the bloodstained truth of the actual battles of his time? If so, we may hear him more as a Bob Dylan or a Bob Marley, responding to very real tensions of the times than as a visionary projecting a future Elysium.

This, after all, was a visceral person who could react quite brutally to close encounters in his own life, whether interruptions or unnecessary inconvenience. We are told that Beethoven frequented a 'cellar' where he sat in a corner of a public room 'beyond the reach of all the chattering and disputation ... drinking wine and beer, eating cheese and red herrings, and studying the newspapers'. But when a stranger sat nearby one evening,

> Beethoven looked hard at him, and spat on the floor as if he had seen a toad; then glanced at the newspaper, then again at the intruder, and spat again, his hair bristling gradually into a more shaggy ferocity, till he closed the alternation of spitting and staring, by fairly exclaiming 'What a scoundrelly phiz!' and rushing out of the room.[36]

Not a man to mince words, Beethoven's response to criticism could be equally direct. The composer let it be known to a critic of the admittedly brash *Wellington's Victory* with its cannon shots, fanfares and national marches, that his own 'shit' was better than anything the critic had come up with.[37]

In a less personal vein, when the Congress of Vienna met in the years 1814 and 1815 to reorganize

---

36 O. G. Sonneck (ed.). *Beethoven: Impressions by his Contemporaries*, p. 114, from a reminiscence by Sir John Russell of a tour undertaken in 1820 and published in Edinburgh in 1828 soon after Beethoven's death.

37 Kinderman *Beethoven*, p. 259.

Europe after Napoleon's first abdication, Beethoven refreshed his opera *Leonora* from a decade earlier, in order to celebrate the promise of the end of war and oppression. In its now third version as *Fidelio*, the music not only celebrated a hopeful replacement of war and oppression by peaceful co-existence, it gave passionate expression to an ideal of married life. We may have no difficulty hearing as an outpouring of Beethoven's sense of what would have brought harmony to his own life if only he had been given a different start, which is to say if only he hadn't been Beethoven.

Then there is the finale in the Ninth, with the words and music leaving us in an ecstasy as if of 'mission accomplished'. But in the symphony itself, the vision of the 'millions' in joy's embrace is imparted only after exposing the audience to hollow despair, followed by some intermittently relieved exuberance that may remind us of that Dionysian frenzy, and this in turn succeeded by an almost unreal vision of peace and harmony. It is only then, and after some backward glances and a glimpse of military frenzy, that we reach that final shout of joy, to which, with its thunderous applause, the audience responds in a recuperative but short-lived ecstasy of its own.

Rather than leapfrogging present nastiness and, as in that supporter song, focusing on the golden day that comes 'at the end of the storm', is it not better, and as has been said, to 'engage with the tension – and occasionally terror – of the present' than focus on a 'beautiful future' when everything is 'gonna [sic] be alright'?[38] Rather the protest song than an imagined

---

38   Corey Seymour, *Vogue Newsletter*, 'Rebel Music: Protest Songs from Beethoven to Bob Marley, to Beyoncé have

future transported unrealistically into the present within the abstracted space-time of a concert hall. Surely that would also be the view of a composer who was exceptionally vulnerable to all-too-little visited parts of the human soul, but able and also passionately concerned to give them musical expression.

Beethoven preoccupation with Schiller's ode from 1785 began already when he was a teenager and caught up in the revolutionary visions of freedom and joy rampant at the time. His return to it nearly three decades later was more measured. A biographer notes that, when going over the text, the composer '[i]n the end ... removed all the most obvious references that mark the *Ode to Joy* as a glorified drinking song, while preserving a series of powerful and direct images with universal social connotations'.[39] Earlier, the passionate engagement in ideals that its images presented had been the reserve of philosophers, who kept the images under intellectual wraps before being unwrapped in the form of banners in the time of revolution. Now they were associated with the miseries of war and occupation and it was necessary, just as that ballet had intimated in its version of the creation of ordinary humans, for a Dionysian strain to be edited out. For Beethoven, the Ode's ideal of fellowship would be as obviously topical for its patent *failure* to be fulfilled as it was to our own world in its local *realization* in Berlin just two centuries later.

At about the time of the 'Emperor' piano concert of 1809, Beethoven had written of a 'destructive, disorderly life' in which he saw and heard 'nothing

been speaking truth to their times and ours.', www.vogue. com, 13 June, 2020.

39   Kinderman, *Beethoven*, p. 302.

but drums, cannons, and human misery in every form ...'. The noise even compelled him to discontinue his singing parties,[40] yes, sing-alongs, held in his rooms. At the time Beethoven could still hear. What we can still hear from ten years later in the drumrolls and fanfares that interrupt the ritual prayer for divine mercy, or redemption, that ends the *Missa Solemnis* is a preoccupation with these harsher realities.

---

40   Swafford, *Beethoven*, p. 528.

10. Human Possibilities

Yes, redemption, how to account for God's forgiveness? Being a bit of a Titan himself, Beethoven in his own dealings with the deity would tend to the admonitory rather than devotional. Although sensitive to what humanity needs, or due to that, what emerges in Beethoven biography suggests that he would be the last person to 'prostrate' himself before any deity, even less so before one promising joy as a reward, as at one place the Ode that he set to music insists.

Yet there were two things Beethoven remained dedicated to, both instilled in him in his early years in Bonn: his family and his talent. These were connected, since the latter had been needed for taking care of the former, even if his insistence later on taking on the guardianship of his nephew Karl was to be a piece of self-help: it gave him a reason not to die at a time when the life-sustaining gift of creativity seemed to have deserted him.[41]

As for that gift, it is also said that it was with an 'ineradicable sense' of his musical talent that he arrived in Vienna at the age of twenty-two, in the firm belief that with its improvement he would 'discover new means of expression', which in his case also meant, as the commentator says, 'new territories of the human'.[42]

---

41   See Swafford, *Beethoven*, p. 665.
42   Ibid., p. 69.

So, yes, talent and the sense of mission that its possession gave him were what Beethoven indeed prostrated himself before. The dedication here was to restitution, his own and that of others here on earth.

That invites a closer look at that song from the musical, 'You'll never walk alone'. It shares in its original setting with the Ninth's *Ode to Joy* a 'universal' association. The only halfway happy resolution in the musical involves holiness, but there is no abject submission to deity. The plot focuses on two ill-starred lovers, one of whom (in the original version) dies by his own hand after a bungled robbery designed to secure money for a family on the way. The song offers the girl hope and the young man, invisibly resurrected, puts a kind of divine seal on it.

The story thus usefully fuses two notions: first the outcast or misfit, for whom politically and morally group affiliations with marriage among them are unavailable and are therefore dismissively grouped among social failures; and secondly, a deprived partner comforted by assurances from 'above' about restoration here on earth.

In neither of these is there any thought of the outcast's loneliness being terminal, or even of it being relieved vicariously in the way that many church hymns and songs from the Southern States celebrate by 'walking with Jesus'. Rather, the thought is a timeless basis for believing that humankind will be able, by itself, to cast aside its self-enforced divisions and reclaim its outcasts and misfits.

So too with Beethoven now in his Ninth, still politically engaged but clear in his mind that the ideals of Enlightenment that sparked the French Revolution will never be furthered by war and entrusted to military or political icons, nor to God:

By way of Schiller's poem, in the Ninth Symphony Beethoven declared that the ideal society, Elysium, was ... something that we must do for ourselves as brothers and sisters, as husbands and wives and as citizens in the brotherhood of humanity.[43]

Beethoven was a misfit but had a place in society due to his musical abilities. We might imagine that without it he would have been just another social delinquent, but then how much of his actual delinquency was due to the talent? He was once arrested as a tramp but that was while deaf and out on the street thinking of his music. Whatever the case, here was an artist unable to 'reconcile himself with the society around him'[44] and living his life ever closer to that ground zero of solitude over which he had hovered from the start and was now the platform for his salvation.

A conventional way out would be to marry. Curiously, he would anticipate van Gogh here too. Both were three times refused. Like the deafness, that must of course have also given added impetus to the talent. The results otherwise would have been disastrous for ourselves and worse for the ladies in question. The more enduring solution to the threat of existential solitude was the space occupied by the talent. He had proved it enough to himself, and it had been confirmed for him by others. But now, as we might say, left to itself, it was there to be honed without him having to think of what others thought of it. The same source writes that '[p]art of his gift

43   Jan Swafford, 'How Beethoven Outgrew his Hero Worship', CNN, 'Opinion, Political Op Eds Social Commentary,' 16 December, 2020.

44   Kelly, OUP Blog, see note 34.

was the *raptus*, that ability to withdraw into an inner world that took him beyond everything and everyone around him, and also took him beyond the legion of afflictions that assailed him. Improvising at the keyboard and otherwise, he found solitude even in company. Solitude his steadiest and most welcome companion.[45]

---

45   Swafford, *Beethoven*, p. 128.

11. The Talent Card

There were living companions too, loyal helpers, willing supporters and long-suffering friends and admirers. Beethoven's ground – that x from which his social identity options radiated – was never quite 'zero'. But support from his circle would not be the kind to provide a sense of human bonding. He was, by all accounts, deaf also in this respect, unable to react to others' happiness or misery in any mutual and communicative manner, whether in joy or sorrow. His only intimate was this ability to find means of musical expression that could express those 'new territories of the human', undiscovered areas where a spiritual element common to ordinary humans, but largely undiscovered by so many of these, could be put into music, that is to say, areas from which they were all-too-ordinarily protected through ossified habits of thought and behaviour.

Creativity is a blank cheque. It can be anything from finding loopholes in the law to cracking the hardest codes. Producing a sketch or painting without a model is creative. Creating a new style by putting ordinary things in a frame and calling it an 'installation' is doubly creative. The continual self-renewal of art is itself creation, even when renewal means destroying or simply negating current styles. In Paris, in the

1960s street artists chalked religious motifs on half the width of sidewalks. These were poor artists, that is to say penniless, hippies even, at least they looked that way and there was a receptacle for coins. The art was imitative, usually in the form of copies of famous paintings and – perhaps (also creatively) to capture more customers – with traditional religious motifs. The presentation too was creative enough in yet another way: it forced pedestrians to file past slowly and choose whether or not to tread on the artwork. That might be sacrilege or even (though perhaps intentional) blasphemy. It would in any case offend the street artist if present.

On being interviewed, one of these had a story to tell. Numbed by the monotony of working on an automobile assembly line in Detroit, he and his workmates interrupted its mind-destroying repetitiveness by ensuring that things sometimes went wrong. An almost completed automobile would be crushed beyond repair, usually on Fridays as a liberating prelude to the weekend release.

A borderline case? Some have discerned destruction in all creativity: it merely upsets a Creation already difficult enough for a sin-laden humanity to keep on a steady course. More pragmatically, others might ask whether we need it. Isn't an absorbing or useful job enough? If solitude is where creativity has its workplace, does that not itself indicate that what it gives rise to must be a symptom of social and even psychological inadequacy? Beethoven's late works were heard as the compositions not merely of someone deaf but of a social derelict out of touch with the realities and possibilities of a normal life.

Or does it just all just down to trying to be different? Perhaps all we need is a capacity to innovate and improvise in order to keep things running and for us to stay on course. Once our inventive skills are no longer geared to social reality, there is nothing to stop this much-lauded creativity from running wild. Beyond providing some mental ventilation at art galleries and in concert halls, along with those lucrative careers in public relations and advertising, it plays no part at all, at least not as far as bringing us closer together socially is concerned. With no integral part to play in consolidating our society, all it does is race impotently like an automobile engine when the clutch and accelerator are pressed simultaneously.

That creativity can be both liberating and constructive seems nevertheless too good an idea to let go of. That doesn't mean we should ignore its negative sides; it has its costs, or to look at it from the other end, it may be a solution to a social deficit just as much as it depends on one. Why be creative unless you need to be? Is creativity perhaps a human right, creative being something we can and should be in order to be whole in ourselves? Are those in whom there are no signs of creativity to be pitied or even cared for? Should they be protected from us or we from them? If a felt need to be creative occurs all too randomly, should we look to the causes, whether psychological or sociological and make the necessary repairs?

The need to be or feel creative may be a symptom of loneliness. The latter can be seen as an extreme case of divisiveness, one that provides no 'we' group other than a notional association of loners, and this can be interpreted as due to a failure of society itself to be adequately (and as with Prometheus 'creatively') infused by yet another Muse, Harmonia. Inclusion of the virtue of concord in the ordinary human make-up would allow creases of loneliness in the social fabric to iron themselves out in normal human activity, that is to say with no special need to be creative in this respect. But what if being socially creative were essential to becoming a whole human being? In that case Harmonia's infusion of concord in the ordinary human would appear as an aim inherent in us all, even if it is one that only social creativity on the part of the individual can achieve. And then, if being a socially creative individual depends on, or is in some way linked with solitude, we can form an idea of social creativity emerging from within the tangled skein of social fabric through the needle of sharpened focus that gives loners insight into what Harmonia's social contribution calls for. If it were also true that being creative was a requirement of *self*-fulfilment, together the flowering of human possibilities being the way to social harmony, then the loner would be playing an essential part in choreographing that final heroic and harmonious dance.

This loner need not appear in the guise of the lonely romantic hero spinning elegies in a garret. More to the task would be one infused with the credo of the Enlightenment that the young Ludwig van Beethoven had absorbed in his twenty-two years in Bonn. Putting terrorists and martyrs to other credos aside, it makes sense to say that a vantage-point outside society, allowing a both critical and edifying stance towards society, provides a chance to see or sense and, in one way or another, express what it seriously lacks.

From an evolutionary perspective, a society's seemingly inevitable ability to exclude or expel some of its members may even, in this way, be its happily creative answer to its own problems. Who knows?

Developing this possibility without commitment to any such article of evolutionary faith, we can see how, in terms of an earlier analogy, the cards we are dealt are not enough to give us all a place in society. We can look at it in this way: in 'lucky' circumstances, in the sense that we have no intimation of anything going wrong, the 'hand' and the hand holding it are indistinguishable. We are products of the basic facts filled out in our birth certificates and those later term reports. We find ourselves not just 'with' but *being* these 'aptitudes tendencies, instincts and passions' and with these influenced in turn by our 'definite surroundings'. We belong to our inheritance and live out of the environment into which, as the philosopher Martin Heidegger puts it, we are 'thrown'.[46] Until, that is, it occurs to us that discarding is part of the game and that some cards in the 'hand' are exchangeable. We now see that the 'hand' and the hand holding it are not identical. But then there is holding hand's shock at finding itself without an identity, no more than a characterless x at the storm centre around which the winds of identity whirl.

Someone dealt a sparse hand when it comes to ordinary social engagement based on home-life and a useful job will be dependent on whatever cards are held. If lucky enough to be dealt a talent, you will want to have it compensate for the cards that are missing. Creativity is a good card to be left with, but will it ever compensate for what the 'hand' lacked?

You might think so: we need only look at the careers of those famous enough for us to know them,

---

46   Martin Heidegger, *Being and Time*, trans. John
      Macquarrie and Edward Robinson, New York: Harper &
      Row, 1962.

especially film and pop stars: early deserting fathers, the need to scrape a living, drug addiction and yet, through determination and some assistance, a name known about as universally as the media age makes possible. Once rescued by a well-received talent, a social derelict at birth abandoned by a father can buy the mother a mansion.

As part of that list of aptitudes etc. with which you are 'thrown', talent is not something you can honestly take personal credit for. Whatever you manage to impress people with by cultivating it will depend on the good fortune that put it into your hands. Unless you remain dim-witted, dishonest or 'lucky' enough to mistake the 'hand' for the hand holding it, you will realize it might not have been given to you. This is something you should bear in mind when doing what you can to develop it. If it means buying a new house for your mother, well and good. You may help a sister or brother out of their troubles too, or a nephew.

As you bask in the glow of your admirers, it should also occur to you that it is to your own advantage that you have honed that gift and may still be honing it. Well, you say, why not? No sense in not chasing your luck, others also benefit and their doing so is part of your success, a nice reciprocity: you owe to them the fruits of what you endured and which also they now enjoy. Yes, indeed, the fact that your success is due not just to others' enjoyment, but to you giving it to them in the first place, is another pat on your back.

But all this being a matter of self-satisfaction jars with the knowledge that *you* have been handed a gift. Even if it is a lucky chance shouldn't you give some thought to the less lucky? Mustn't someone or something, or simply everyone, be thanked for such a favour and it helping you out of a sticky situation? God, for example? That talent may have been meant for more than just yourself.

Redemption. It has been a long time coming.

12. Sisyphus and 'Soulitude'

According to the orthodox line, redemption is a form of recovery in which God has given us a plan for how it is to be done, a blueprint published in a teaching delivered in a model performance of how it should be put into practice. There is a lot about abstinence, little about insight and almost nothing that closes a gap between social delinquency and what is owed to society. But those who, like Beethoven, are unable to be 'reconciled' with their society[47] are more likely than others to be victims of those societies than debtors needing to make amends. Nevertheless, someone forced to a life ever closer to the ground zero of solitude and given a creative ability is better placed than most to see the need of such a plan.

Reconciliation with the kind of society he found himself in was not on Beethoven's mind. On the contrary, he seems to have seen and felt to his core all that it lacked. It is from this outsider's vantage-point in his own society that we can glimpse the psychology that allows it to be said of him that 'to the end [he] called himself a servant of humanity'.[48].

Beethoven's own thoughts on how to compensate for the missing cards whose absence the cultivation

---

47   Kelly, OUP Blog, see note 34.
48   Swafford, *Beethoven*, p. 77.

of that talent merely increased, was to speak both to and for the failed humanity around him. Rather than compensation for his own isolation, in view of what he felt this creative talent was destined for, it would be an added burden, his. A vision of humanity saved is that of a journey completed, but creativity has no ideal stopping point. Its products disappear at birth as though one's children were being adopted away one after the other. When so central, as in the cases of a van Gogh or Beethoven, and of course a thousand others, any even temporary loss of creativity can cause panic and bring thoughts of suicide. Close to the natural end of his own life, Beethoven's solicitude for his nephew tided him over one of his own traumatically barren periods.

Continual creation is an ideal that, in its constantly insipient failure, can become a form of compulsion and part of creativity's pathology. It is Sisyphean in never reaching a point of saturation where the job is done. As in an addiction, if not actually being one, in a creative spell new projects must stand in line, not for the money but for the soul. A *curriculum vitae* of opus numbers provides no closure. The driving force for someone left with a talent is the hope of filling a void that will never be filled. We might call it 'soulitude', the lot of souls that are lost to themselves, empty but waiting every moment for inspiration and a refill from that creative spirit. But this void will never be filled and creation to date never does creativity justice. If nothing new or better comes along, well that too prompts despair.

Exaggeration? Yes, it seems clear that Beethoven enjoyed developing his talent. It must have taken his mind off worries both mundane and existential. Listening to the humour, exuberance and sheer exhilaration in the music of the 'early' and 'middle periods, it is easy to sense a corresponding enthusiasm and self-confirmation in the composing. Maybe not as rapt as when improvising in the company of solitude, his true companion, but neither here nor anywhere else in Beethoven's life in Vienna do we get a sense of someone losing touch with himself.

True, but that isn't the point. There is that constant mission. Think back to *The Creatures of Prometheus*. Everyone including Apollo takes part in the finale's heroic dance but the dance itself is led by two newly created humans. That is the point. The redemption of human beings is up to themselves. It is they who must give it. Among the Muses that programmed Prometheus's clay 'dummies' with intellect and science were three who gave them music. Social harmony seems to be something they had to deal with by themselves. Had their number included Harmonia, it would have been included, but together with its fragility.

According to myth, at her marriage to Cadmus, son of Agenor, king of Phoenicia, a ceremony attended by all the Olympian gods, Harmonia was given a necklace by her mother Aphrodite. It had been made by Hephaestus, the God of fire, and would expose their descendants to all sorts of misfortune and tragedy. Yes, another version of the Garden of Eden. Snakes and necklaces are not all that different and the one might do service for the other. Perhaps the Bible stole original sin from the Greeks. As it is, any innate sense of social harmony that we find in our own beginnings as a pattern for paradise disappears in the discord that is the name of our daily game. All that is left is that vision of all peoples holding hands and singing the same song, the empty vision of a single society, which being single would also be empty.

From marriage breakdown to international trade boycotts and bitter conflict between political parties, we need no reminding of the disunities that disgrace every sector of human life. Pay disputes, economically motivated warfare, along with messianic terrorism, brutal beheadings, racist discrimination, all of this is daily news. We may wonder just how more distant any ideal of universal fellowship can become.

How would a Beethoven respond to this today? With hearing still intact would he find something of the Ode to Joy in a football crowd singing 'You'll Never Walk Alone?' We can take another look at its provenance. It has to do with a carnival barker called Billy Bigelow.

Like Beethoven, Billy is only loosely linked to his world, in his case by temperament rather than circumstance. His job of calling on passers-by to join in the fun of a travelling carnival can take him anywhere, if only in this case within the confines of 1870s New England. In spite of his job and an aversion to commitment, he falls for Julie, a poor millworker who has come to the show. Fired from his job by the carousel's jealous owner, and Julie fired from hers by her boss for being out too late, they marry and both penniless, to Billy's unexpected joy she becomes pregnant. Prompted by his low-life friend, Jigger, an arranged hold-up and street robbery goes wrong. In the show Billy takes his own life, but the film has him accidentally falling on the knife intended to scare the victim. Grieving, Julie is reminded of a song by a cousin and begins singing: 'when you walk through a storm, hold your head up high, and don't be afraid of the dark'. The cousin takes over and sings 'You'll Never Walk Alone'.

With the mess of his own making behind him, and placed now in a timeless limbo short of heaven polishing stars, Billy has things to put right. An opportunity for redemption comes in due course as a stand-in St. Peter called 'Starkeeper' grants him a day back on earth to take care of those he has left behind. Earthly things having rolled on in time, his daughter Louise is now a teenager and not unlike her father in being a free spirit in the earthier sense. Due to his history, she becomes also a social outcast. Unseen, he sees his spirited daughter frozen out by her colleagues. She and her class, at an end-of-term graduation, are told they must forget whatever good or bad their parents have done and go on to make their own lives. The speaker, Dr. Seldon but to us visible as the stand-in St. Peter, calls on them to sing 'You'll Never Walk Alone'. At first Louise is hesitant, but on Billy urging her she joins in, as does his widowed wife Julie, also attending, on being invisibly assured that he loved her.[49]

Billy is doubtless now in Heaven or Elysium. Is he singing too? Up there we cannot hear him and it doesn't matter. Singing together and dancing are analogies. They occur in time and mark a recovery here on earth, the realization of a goal that we somehow already have it in ourselves to cherish, though typically without realizing it until our own way of 'being together' is threatened.

Billy's redemption is personal, but that is also analogy. Although mediated by someone 'in the know', and however invisibly, it is still his own doing.

---

49   *Carousel*, 1945 musical by Richard Rogers (music) and Oscar Hammerstein (libretto) adapted from *Liliom* by Ferenc Molnár.

To mend matters, all he needed was some hard nudging and encouragement. The invisibility along with Billy's churlish yet inquiringly flexible 'find out for myself' point of view transform the character into a representative of a humankind that has dropped the protection of self-made myths. *Carousel* tells an Enlightenment story that, if presented with a libretto for a ballet, Beethoven himself might have set to music.

What would the narrative say? It could tell us of the rigidity of a social structure based on a narrow sense of morality that sees universal harmony as a matter of cancelling the differences in which any initial sense of belonging is formed. Instead of the real abstraction of an individual looking with complacency, or in either horror or time-saving and option-retaining irony, at the hand dealt by time and location, and then facing or turning a back on the hard choice between making personal capital out of it and devoting one's lot to 'humanity', here humanity has become an abstraction. A real humanity has been shaved of its basic identity-giving differences.

Not far from the Anfield stadium, where supporters on both sides might sing 'You'll Never Walk Alone', lies the downtown Cavern Club where, in the 1960s, the Beatles provided society with something to soften the brittle surface of a world covering its sores with a return to pre-war proprieties and now awakened to the threat of atomic warfare. Their creative popular music spoke to a younger generation of the worries, hopes and joys of everyday life. Then the 1990s saw the arrival of a music tradition with a more radical, sweeping and literally 'cavernous' approach to ingrown proprieties.

'Metal' disputes the very idea of humanism and not just its comforting reliance on science in realizing innate ideals of togetherness. It looks at death and evil in the face and even takes their side, if only to give them more space in our lives than we usually like. The cult of Satan isn't even enough, since by merely inverting the Judaeo-Christian value scale so many of us have been brought up with, it still accepts its terms. Further back, with darker rules, are the Celts and further still the mythical beginnings of our symbolic gods. Brought into the present they become the occult.

Ideological, and with footnotes on Nietzsche, concerned as it is with guiding beliefs and ideals to do with community, 'metal' has little effect outside its own expanding circles other than by generating a layer of glowing magna beneath the stolid tectonics of a self-perpetuating society. It is a kind of protest but not unlike that of those workers who, in an undetected and more literally metal but unmusical protest trashed an automobile once in a while to unsettle an endless routine. It helped them to stay on the job, at least until one of them chose to become a sidewalk decorator. As with all creativity, metal ceaselessly re-invents itself on that lower screen ticker text that scrolls away while the slow-motion picture above remains unaffected and, with it, our daily lives.

Not only that, unsurprisingly, under its series of labels (black, trash, speed, death, melodic, symphonic, ambient, avant-garde), metal with its constant re-invention of itself engages in its own subterranean identity politics. If the urge here is to make a name, and not necessarily more money (itself a creative enough innovation in our society), and although some self-styled Satanist innovators have burned churches and worse, in its harsh and grating way the ability of this deeper musical dig into the mystery of being remains musical for ears attuned to its sound and ethos. That its special slot is still within earshot of the many is epitomized by a suitably named blogger who introduces a review of a new disc 'Demonic Resurrection' with 'Ladies and gents, it's time to get demonic'.[50]

50   Mark Angel Brandt, 'Blog of Putrefaction' @Putrid Blog, Britain's Metal Underground.

13. Testing Existence

Commercial and psychological motives in constant interaction prevent everyday access to dimensions of human existence that solitude can reveal. It is a 'luxury' that subterranean cultures can allow themselves. For others, a night out on the demonic, with its immersion in scenarios dusted off and restored from humanity's less civilized beginnings, might remind those who know him of Wagner. Even if it fails to provide an awakening of the kind that inspires 'new ways of looking at the world', as Nick Cave puts it in lamenting the stifling effect of a popular and media-fed cult of political correctness, it at least allows a glimpse of a place from where fixtures in our way of life, some of them sacred, appear as 'wheezes' that humanity itself has come up with throughout history in the cause of securing or heightening its own status. We may gain from that fleeting vantage point some flash of insight into why cosmic ignorance about humanity's status in nature is itself something we prefer to ignore.

As for 'Metal' music in all its guises, with its constant re-invention and proliferation of styles, the chances are that it will continue to figure on that rapidly rolling ticker text and be, given the extent of its retro-engagement with the politics of life, an ever-active variable in some guise or other.

According to the nineteenth-century thinker cited earlier, a genius works in the opposite direction, retracing the past and adding something new, possibly radically so. The point itself is made in a radical way is still within a Judaeo-Christian frame. The genius is said 'consciously [to begin] just as primitively as did Adam' and 'every time a genius is born, existence is at it were put to the test'.[51]

Much music might be said to test existence. But to begin with Adam means accepting the Bible story or else some earlier version as that of Harmonia's fateful necklace. The *idea* of a unified humanity is there from the start, but it quickly becomes prey to situations caused by a less than harmonious package of programmes inherited from other and not always reliable Muses.

In retracing the history of European music, Beethoven had a vision of a fulfilled human life for all constantly before him. Born, as he was, to find himself uniquely gifted but socially deprived, his late works were composed in the solitude of a 'lockdown' that immunised him from the existential blindness that a wider coverage of an everyday world so easily induces. That Beethoven here puts existence to the test for us all is something those attuned to his music may well feel. A pianist has said that working with music that was 'to such a degree honest and wants to go somewhere' had changed him.[52] The creativity itself is infectious, something we are the more likely to experience, the

---

51 Søren Kierkegaard, *The Concept of Anxiety: A Simple Psychologically Oriented Deliberation in View of the Dogmatic Problem of Hereditary Sin*, trans. Alastair Hannay, New York: Liveright/W.W. Norton, 2014, p. 127.

52 Leif Ove Andsnes, 'En Indre Glød'. Intervju', *Klassekampen*, Oslo, 31 December, 2020, p. 14.

greater the situation calls for or permits absorption as in the current pandemic, and who can be more absorbed than the pianist performing the music? Another pianist writes:

> with a near-total upending of our daily lives, it was perhaps inevitable that, alongside a reassessment of our own plans and priorities, we had begun to listen to Beethoven with different ears. ... To be clear, Beethoven needed and needs no reassessment. His music is immortal and inextricably interwoven with humanity's heritage. For so many of us, he is as obvious as air. He belongs to a tiny handful of timeless giants who make us cheer in wonder or fall silent in disbelief, so unreachable they are in the blazing radiance of their genius. And yet he can make us love and accept ourselves that little bit more, simply for belonging to the same humankind as him.[53]

Some misleading implications of these superlatives need neutralizing. It can sound as though Beethoven were superhuman. He has indeed been placed too long on a pedestal beyond normal reach and though quite short and stocky, made to look much larger than life with a flowing poet's hairstyle. In his oration at the funeral, the playwright Franz Grillparzer spoke of Beethoven as a composer who none would surpass, but that was because Grillparzer saw a dangerous break with music's 'authentic' classical tradition in the way Beethoven's music had developed. Things seriously musical were to stop with Beethoven; if what he had started went further it would not be music.

---

53   'Every note pulses with life and warmth: pianist Boris Giltburg on Beethoven's Music, *The Guardian*, 27 December, 2020.

Quite otherwise with Schubert. He thought Beethoven had done everything he had been thinking of doing himself. The point, however, is that Beethoven, by not becoming a romantic composer and having a talent immunized from any immediate connection with his life's daily ups and downs, could become a very human musical representative of ordinary human beings. The joy of 'An die Freude' declaimed in the Ninth Symphony need not be that of a single society suspended from its daily travails in the socially hermetic frame of a concert hall; it can be the thrill that anyone or everyone there can feel of the fulfilment of a hope that Beethoven himself once put into words, that he be given 'but one day of pure joy'.[54]

Anything deserving to be called a test of existence must surely call for an appreciation not only of the distance between its needs and hopes but also of the indeterminate gap between hope and fulfilment. The test is whether we have the strength of mind, along with whatever else is required, to accept that fulfilment is nevertheless within human range.

What that means for our investigation into the relation between subjectivity and creativity is not as clear as *we* might have hoped. But if one thing stands out, it is that creativity appears in many shapes and sizes. It can be exceedingly trivial. Take seemingly accidental word association. Here, our first section's heading's 'askancing' could be an unwittingly witty allusion to a popular Swedish television show familiar to the author, 'Allsang på Skansen'. The latter term is the name of an open-air museum on an island where the

---

54   See Swafford, *Beethoven*, p. 843, where the connection is made with this plea to 'Providence' in the Heiligenstadt Testament.

sing-along is televised before an audience. Wordplay is an ability we all have and one that Beethoven himself displays extensively in his conversation books, often as labels for his friends and associates. Creativity, when it fails, can be creatively assisted through techniques that jolt it into action. Scriptwriters of long-standing television series need such second-order creativity to keep their first-order creativity alive. These days, creativity is often connected (creatively?) with smart moves, or 'dodges', that preserve the spirit but not the letter of some inconvenient regulation.

Subjectivity is similarly protean, in general it is just a notion we use to distinguish a focus on what goes on in the conscious mind and what happens 'out there' regardless of who pays attention. Here a distinction has been made within that wider meaning: solitude as opposed to loneliness. The former is where home truths about being a human can come to roost, the latter a sense of wanting to return to the good old home one knows. Those with a special talent may face and survive their solitude by bringing 'humanity' within its embrace. For a worn-out Vincent van Gogh, it was to console a humanity seen in the light of early failures and suffering. Solitude in Ludwig van Beethoven's case was largely due to his talent, but both in combination were devoted to a humanity the pain of whose failure to live up to its ideals seems to have been one that he was able himself to feel.

Just two instances, but they exemplify a dynamic in which visions of a unified humanity appear that are inaccessible to politicians confined to the 'we' embrace of a party programme. There they appear as empty slogans with which partisan political ways and means can sound suitably universal. Claims on behalf of the exploited and oppressed when amplified in the media disseminate a 'we'-thinking that allows long victimized sections of society and, with slavery, whole populations much needed identity. By being politically visible, they can be restored to their original dignities. Political and purely human effort can be used to heal those injustices where racism and inherently psychologically caused views of group inferiority are concerned. But as one of our sources has said, 'its once honourable attempt to reimagine our society in a more equitable way', the cult of correctness 'now embodies all the worst aspects that religion has to offer'.[55]

In a 'cancel culture' we find a media-assisted populist inquisition that victimizes those, and especially public figures, who venture to question an erasure of the past in order to be able to treat everyone as 'one of us'. Its own 'evil' is to prohibit the probing of 'difficult ideas'. Among these, from what has been said here, is the dependence of human beings on a nurturing context in which individual humans can become 'selves in society' but also sensitive enough to their own dependence on their background to be able to see for themselves the need, or else to be jerked into seeing it by some talented outcast. It is, according to our source, 'both the function and glory of art and ideas' to do so'.

The historian tells of Plato describing a human being as a 'featherless biped', at which Diogenes the Cynic being present plucked the feathers from a cockerel and, pointing to it, said 'here is Plato's man'.[56]

---

55   Cave, see note 14.
56   Diogenes Laërtius, *Lives and Opinions of the Eminent Philosophers*, trans. Charles Duke Konge, Whitefish MT: Kessinger Publishing, Bk. 3, 2006.

Looked at in evolutionary terms, the image has some appeal: natural selection has at least, if not deprived us of a natural 'habit', failed to give us any. It has also left us looking for a habitat. We are ready to applaud our creativity in providing the former but less so with the latter. That neither nature nor God has favoured us with a cover for our social nakedness, a home and heritage, is harder to swallow than being left to provide our own feathers. But we can be even more reluctant to contemplate that God's provision of a home may be a matter of our own creativity rather than God's. It is after all a rather simple idea and maybe just a bit too convenient.

Maybe so, but what is forgotten – and we try to keep forgetting – is the context of what gave us our own sense of belonging, a sense that in a solitude that is enforced or induced we are made to recover. Not by its being revealed in any special guise, but rather by our being able to plumb these depths of the human situation sufficiently to detect the pathological status of much of what we call culture, and more particularly the unquestioned habits of thought and practice with which we cover our own and humanity's initially inherent nakedness.

Epilogue

Well, how did it go?

'A lot of undressing there but sing-along seems to have gone with it.'

Well, the word brings many analogies and associations to mind. It's just as well to pinpoint the less attractive before having them spoil the fun.

'All this about political correctness bringing evil to light only to add more – it sounded as if you were having your own inquisitorial beef when sing-alongs are really just harmless attempts to imitate the birds.'

Hardly, really to imitate the birds, our brains would have to be born with social media implants.

'All right, but you mentioned pandemics, what of those balcony sing-alongs that bring neighbours out of solitary in a way that would hardly happen otherwise?

No solution there. They remind me of those sad prisoners let out for a short breather in the middle of Beethoven's *Fidelio*. The same goes for those alleged on-line sing-alongs with thousands ... just a moment of relief.

'O.K. but, talking of Beethoven, there was something about French cannons putting a stop to Ludwig van's singing parties? Anything wrong with these?'

The cannons or the singing? Or both? Maybe some history will help.

'Again, all ears ...'

Right, to celebrate the Soviet victory at Stalingrad in February 1943 Stalin decided 'The Internationale' had to be replaced with something suitable for celebrating a nation's prowess. It would have to be ready by November for the still vital Revolution celebrations, so a competition was arranged and forty melodies out of more than two hundred submissions put to a jury. The judges chose a piece by a professor from the music conservatory who happened to be an old friend of Stalin, and he, Josef Stalin, with his classically tuned musicality was broad-minded enough to take a 'decadent' modernist Shostakovich out of the cold to provide the orchestration.[57] With Stalin's demise, and to cut all connection with the Soviet past, Yeltsin wanted another melody, a popular one by the Russian composer Glinka. Being wordless, it left winning ice hockey teams frustratingly mute, but with the populist idol Putin's arrival on the scenes, that past had to be restored as part of the national heritage. You can't have hiatuses in a heritage. So the old melody came back with a new text by the original lyricist. Anthems can tend, in this way, to keep in step with 'homeland' politics: the Australian anthem was recently re-texted to include an indigenous heritage by almost inaudibly changing the words 'young and free' to 'one and free'. Yes, along with the usual asides to 'glory' the Russian anthem now spoke in terms palatable to practically anyone. Except for the French, most people will be happy to sing of their 'sacred state' under 'God's protection' and to dwell with domestic warmth on

---

57   Some details here are from Jan Roar Bjørkvold, 'Den store nasjonalhymnen [The Great National Anthem]', *Klassekampen*, Oslo,30 December, 2020, pp. 10-11.

a 'homeland' with its 'age-old union of fraternal peoples'. The melody itself was so catching that even Swedish supporters unlettered in Russian are said to have minded less about losing ice hockey matches to their neighbour.

'But by posing as a populist's Tsar, wasn't Putin just taking it all back to a Hobbesian free-for-all where those close to this Leviathan come off best?'

That may be true of today's Russia, but at least they don't incarcerate people who sing their anthem improperly as in China. If a guideline is needed here, or some principle, maybe the best we can do is something like this: Steer clear of two opposite dystopias, one where you are ID-entified in the register as, at home, a cipher of interest only as lawbreaker and when abroad to be protected even by force as a flag waver, and the other where your every social move is scripted with no adlibbing allowed. In neither of these is there provision for a society's soul and creative spirit: that essential individual.

'From what you have been saying, it seems only misfits and artists have what it takes.'

Well, no, in societies so-called that come close to these dystopian alternatives, we must rely on others ready to tackle victimization in the system. But there must also be recognition of the restorative value of dissent, protest and vision in those whose failure to be reconciled with the system lets them see it and themselves in a both wider and deeper perspective, these also being two sides of the same thing.

'And what is *that* same thing?'

Put it in this way: people generally prefer the framework in which they carry on their lives to be secure enough for them to 'do their own thing'. It can be fostering a talent or bringing up a family or both if circumstances allow. Authoritarian regimes play to this preference by guaranteeing that security. As long as their economies sustain a framework that reduces victimization to a significant low, only those looking for something more exciting and 'creative' will be left out. They can form a subculture without much pressure to become a counter-culture.

According to a Chinese artist and activist now living in the West, any tendency to individual initiative in addressing a society's structure tends to be anaesthetized by the 'comfort of oppression'. People locked in an 'authoritarian mind-set' reinforced by the 'efficiency' and the show' put on by their custodians, bathe happily in a sense of power emanating down from those for whom they have an inborn respect.[58] They avoid any test of their social potential as individuals simply because they don't feel any need for it. If active social wills are seen as essential to human being, it is redundancy in a negative sense. Humans are being kept in a state of social infancy. For the Chinese, this mind-set can be sheer habit grounded in centuries of a Confucianism that gave them a stable domicile governed by wisdom from above. For Western

---

58   Ai Weiwei, Chinese artist and activist, *The Guardian*, 11 January 2021, with current China and Germany his examples: ' "Germany is a very precise society. Its people love the comfort of being oppressed. In China, too, you see that. Once you're used to it, it can be very enjoyable. ... ' You mean there is no room for individuality?' "Yes. They have a different kind of suit: it doesn't look like what they wore in the 1930s, but it still has the same kind of function. They identify with the cult of that authoritarian mindset".'

societies, where the Divine Right of Kings once had the same role but with a nation's self-protection rather than wisdom its charter, the comfort of oppression 'came out' as what it can now widely be seen to be, namely subjection to charismatic or self-assertive and power-based leadership. The comforts it offers are to the humiliated as well as to those who get to share in the material comforts of those in control. Outcasts, the socially deprived, become empowered and their social and political impotence or immaturity is converted into superiority overnight. Fascism is born.

'Yes, but what, once more, after all this, is that "one thing"?'

You and me, or what we need to be, the essential human being, you, me, the individual, becoming my and your essential self by becoming essential to society – not society as such, or the one society, but to my society and to yours, by being similarly essential in each ...

'I think I get the drift, a tall order, even unlikely ...'

Let's hope not.

'I'll sing to that.'

Then let me join you ...

---

www.ingramcontent.com/pod-product-compliance
Lightning Source LLC
Chambersburg PA
CBHW070342100426
42812CB00005B/1398